Guitar Music Theory

Tips and Tricks to Guitar Mastery

Ethan Hayes

TABLE OF CONTENTS

Introduction 1

Chapter 1: Understanding your Guitar 3

Parts of the Guitar 3

Types of Guitars 6

Tuning Your Guitar 8

Proper Position for holding the Guitar 9

Fingering and Using a Pick 10

Chapter 2: Guitar Fretboard and Scales 14

Notes on the Fretboard 14

Half-Steps, Whole-Steps, and Intervals 18

Guitar Scales Every Beginner Must Know 21

Intervals 30

Names and Structure of Intervals 32

What Every Guitarist Must Know 36

Chapter 3: Chords and Chord Progression 38

Understanding Chords 38

Chords Theory and Construction 39

Chord Progressions 51

CAGED Guitar System 53

Chapter 4: More on Chords **58**

Chord Voicing 58

Chord Inversion 61

Power Chords 74

Circle of Fifths.. 82

The Order of Sharps and Flats...................................... 84

Benefits of the Circle of Fifths 85

Chapter 5: Essential Guitar Techniques...............................**87**

Strumming...87

Basic Guitar Strumming Patterns 89

String Muting and Damping 93

Alternate Picking 99

Sharps and Flats 101

Chapter 6: Advanced Techniques – Arpeggios **106**

Using Arpeggios...106

Essential Arpeggio Techniques.....................................115

Chapter 7: Soloing **118**

Soloing Over Chord Progressions 120

Using Arpeggios in Guitar Solos 124

Conclusion **127**

Moving On From Here... 127

References **128**

Introduction

If you have started reading this book with the intention of mastering your guitar skills, then I believe that congratulations are in order. Welcome to one of the most exciting things you can do with your time. You can be sure of a thrilling experience as you continue to expand your knowledge of guitar music production.

The guitar is a popular instrument and has been so for many centuries now. Perhaps the reason we have not been able to do without it is because of the unique feel it brings to the music played on it. Guitar techniques have evolved considerably over the years, making the guitar one of the most sophisticated musical instruments ever. Sometimes, a piece of music isn't complete without the guitar in it. At other times, all that is needed to make a beautiful piece of music is just the guitar. As you continue to learn, you'll discover why that is so.

What then is the best way to learn how to play the guitar? It is not enough to pick up the guitar and plunge yourself straight into learning. Instead, it is more important to understand the theoretical concepts behind what you play and then begin in the right order and work your way through to mastery. In essence, having an overview of the entire journey will help you navigate the learning process better. Besides, chances are you'll learn faster when you are equipped with a theoretical understanding of important concepts. It makes your journey clearer, with each milestone serving as a benchmark to measure your progress. Even if you have outgrown the amateur stage, you will find this approach is still helpful. This way, you are unlikely to skip any important stage of learning. Many people pick up the guitar and give it up too soon because of frustration and lack of a clear direction. For some other people, it is because they are trying to learn with the wrong learning methods. While there are quick tips to get you started, you can't ignore the basics, especially if you hope to create a unique sound.

A number of approaches are used to learn the guitar. Playing the guitar is dynamic, and you may want to choose a tea you may want to choose a teacher who is interested in our style of music. However, a successful approach would be a subjective one. The rules and techniques are not cast in stone. Whether you decide to stick to video tutorials or e-books, engage the service of a one-on-one teacher or rely totally on the self-taught technique, you'll basically need to keep an open mind and maintain a keen interest throughout. More times than not, strong self-motivation is the most important recipe for success in anything.

In this book, the guitar theory course has been segmented into chapters and sections. In each section, key concepts and theories are discussed. At the end of each chapter, the learner is given a summary of important tips. This course also contains enough practice exercises with graphics for visualization, though I encourage you to experiment beyond this book as there are many useful books that can help you. Throughout the course, I emphasize the need to develop the grit to study on your own, because this is the best way to get creative. As with almost every kind of learning, you can use your tutor's guidelines to create your own unique guitar sound, but I encourage not to limit yourself. Anyway, for now, you are not alone on this journey because the process outlined in this book will be simple to follow. You may skip the rudiments if you already have a grasp of them, but I encourage you to still glance through them. In order to ensure you get the best out of the lessons, I suggest getting a guitar of your own. This enables you to follow carefully and immediately experiment using what you have learned.

Once again, welcome to this exciting journey.

Chapter 1

Understanding your Guitar

Parts of the Guitar

The most basic challenge for a beginner who has little or no experience with the instrument he has bought is usually understanding the different parts of the instrument and how best to handle it. Here are the parts of a guitar.

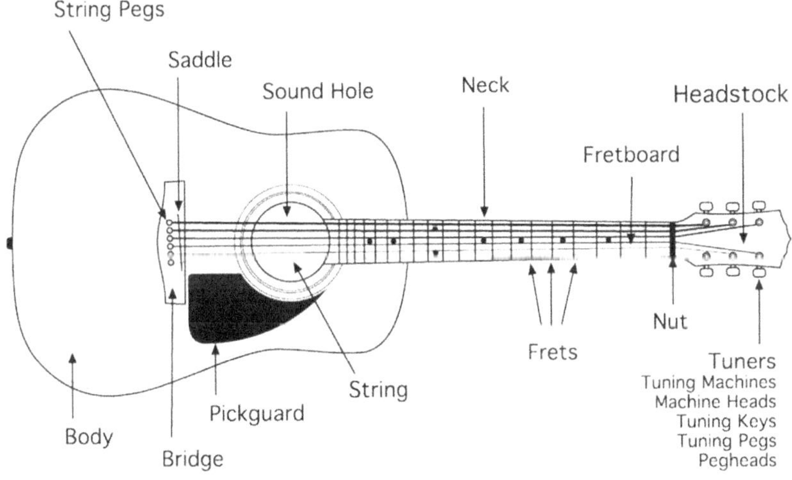

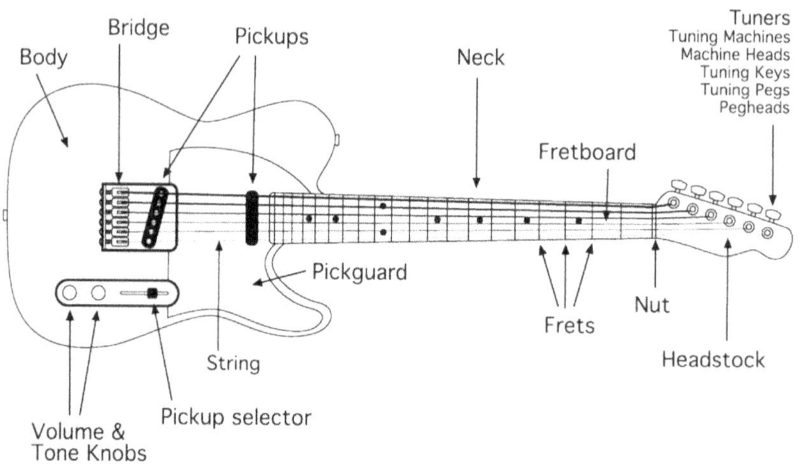

The Headstock

This is the tapered end of the guitar, where the peg heads or tuning machine heads are found.

Tuning Pegs

These are the little peg-like screws positioned around the headstock; they are also known as tuners, tuning keys, pegheads, or machine heads and are used to tune the guitar.

Neck

This is the entire length of the guitar between the box and the headstock, where you see the strings. You hold the strings down on the neck when playing to create chords.

Nut

This is the thin white plastic material located at the end of the neck, just before the headstock. It runs vertically across the neck, forming a little bridge.

Frets

These are the little vertical metal bumps along the neck of the guitar. The spacing is deliberate so that a chromatic scale is built along the neck. When a string is pressed against a fret, it creates a specific note.

Fretboard

This is the space in front of the neck, where the frets are positioned.

Strings

These are the tiny strings that run, along the neck, from the bridge to the headstock. Each string produces a specific sound when pressed or picked, and they vary in thickness from the first to the last. In an acoustic or electric guitar, the strings are six in number but five in a bass guitar. Some may be of nylon, while others will be of wound metal.

The Bridge

This a strong piece of wood or metal, as in electric guitars, which anchors the strings. It is found on the body of the guitar.

Bridge Pins/String Pegs

The pins hold the strings in place on the bridge. The strings run from the bridge to the body of the guitar. These can be removed when the strings need to be replaced.

Saddle

This is at the base of the guitar and strings rest on it, before being pinned to the bridge. All strings make contact with the bridge.

Sound Hole

This the circular hole in the body of the guitar that gives the guitar its sound. To magnify the sound of the guitar, a microphone is positioned near the sound hole. On an electric guitar, a Single Coil Pickup and a Volume button is used to achieve sound magnification.

Pick Guard

It shields the surface of the guitar from scratches, especially when strumming. It is made of plastic, and the colors can be changed according to preference.

Body

The big hollow base or solid base (in electric versions).

Strap Pin

Located at the spine or side of the body, and used for holding the guitar strap.

Electric Guitar

Pickup Selector Switch

It is used to select or switch between different pickups. At most, two pickups can be selected per time.

Volume Control Button

It is used to control the level of the volume.

Tone Knobs

It is used to control the tone texture of the instrument.

Types of Guitars

There are quite a number of varieties. Essentially, we can narrow the names of the type of guitar down to the popular versions, especially the conventional guitar types. Choosing a guitar type is important as this will need to go with the type of music you want to play.

Although this is not the focus of the book, let's make mention of a few;

- **The Bass Guitar** - has 4 thick strings and produces heavier or deeper sounds

- **Acoustic Guitar** - has 6 strings, usually made of wood. Acoustic guitars arc the most portable kind of guitars available. Unlike most guitar types, it does not necessarily require electricity.

- **Electric Guitars** - basically an electronic variant of the acoustic guitar. They have six strings too and a few extra features, such as volume and pickup controls.

- **Weird Guitar** - it's a metal guitar with 7 strings; also electric.

- There are many other variants, counting up to 10 strings and more.

Throughout the course of this book, we will be making reference to two types of guitars: the bass guitar and acoustic or lead guitar (electric version). However, the majority of examples and practice exercises will be based on the acoustic guitar. The main difference between the bass and acoustic guitar is that the former has 4 strings while the latter has 6 strings. Also, the bass guitar has thicker strings, and the sound produced is different.

Tuning Your Guitar

Unless you have a well-tuned guitar, you cannot produce the right sounds, and this is where frustration usually begins. However, tuning is easy to do. In fact, there are three ways you can get your guitar tuned. At first, it may seem difficult, but it gets easier and seamless by continuous practice, as you train your ear.

First, you can use a pitch pipe or tuning fork to tune your guitar. This is how it works. The pitch pipes are available with six different pipes, with each pipe having a unique sound that corresponds to the sound of each string on your guitar. So, when you sound each pipe, you tune the corresponding string with the aid of the machine heads or pegs, until you get the same sound as the pitch pipe. Repeat this for all the strings by sounding the corresponding pipes. At the end of this exercise, you should have a perfectly tuned guitar, ready for playing. Tighten strings to produce a higher sound, loosen them to produce a lower sound.

Second, a piano may be used. Please see the illustration below for guidance. As the illustration shows, all you need to do is press each key, then tune the corresponding guitar string to sound the same as the note from the keyboard.

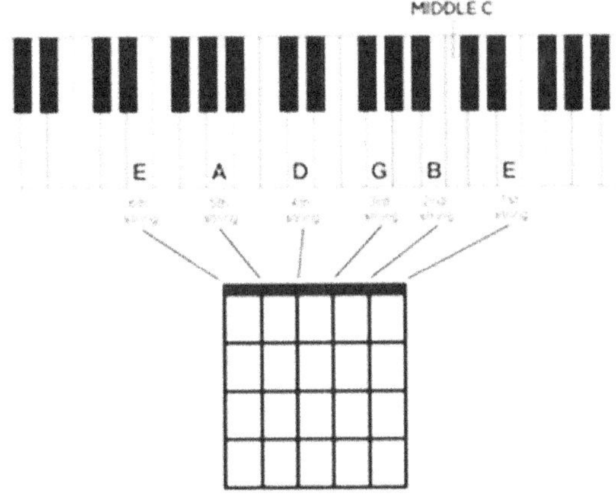

Alternatively, you can always rely on this third method. With your left index finger, hold down the 6th string just behind the 5th fret (remember the frets are the vertical metal strips that line the neck of the guitar and count from the nut backward), and sound the string with your right thumb. That's more of the note produced. Now strike the 5th string while still holding the 6th string. Tune either the 6th or 5th string until they sound alike. Once done, repeat the same procedure with the 5th string held down, and the 4th string sounded open (i.e., without holding the string). Continue also to the 4th string. When you get to the 3rd string, hold it down behind the 4th fret instead of the 5th, then play the 2nd string open. On the 2nd string, return to the 5th fret and play the 1st string open.

Note: the trick here is to ensure that each pair of strings sounds the same (i.e., the notes must be the same).

With continued practice, you'll get the hang of it. This is the most natural way to tune your guitar.

Proper Position for holding the Guitar

The importance of maintaining the right position cannot be overemphasized. The reason for this is that in the long run, the best position helps you play better. Wrong positions lead to fatigue on the wrist and waist, and in the fingers. Refer to the illustrations below for clarity. Beginners may not see the difference in keeping to the positions, but they are as important as every other thing is, especially if you aspire to become a professional player.

- The guitar should rest on your thigh with the end tilted upwards.

- Sit upright and do not slouch.

- Your right arm rests on top of the guitar body for support.

- Your left elbow should hang naturally downwards.

- The left fingers should grip the fretboard without wrapping them around the neck of the guitar.

- Relax your muscles when you feel strain in your wrist or fingers

Note: your fingernails need to be trimmed, at least the fingers you play with. Otherwise, you can't hold down or strike the strings properly.

Fingering and Using a Pick

This is another critically essential fundamental for every guitar player, especially beginners. There are rules that must be adhered to.

Left Finger

Your thumb is for support. It naturally grips the back of the fretboard and gives support to the wrist. The index finger is the first finger, the middle finger is the second finger, the ring finger is the third finger, and the pinky finger is the fourth finger. These are the fingers you use for holding down strings against the fretboard. Ideally, the tip of the finger should press firmly on the strings right behind the frets.

Right Finger

On the right hand, things are a little different; the first four-fingers, including the thumb, are the active fingers; and letters are used for identification, instead of numbers. The letters used for the right hand are derived from Spanish words: *pulgar* for the thumb, *indicio* for the index finger, *medio* for the middle finger, and *anular* for the ring finger. The strings are numbered 1-6, from the bottom up. Strings 1-3 are the light or treble strings, while 4-6 are the bass strings. In the subsequent chapter, you will see how to use your fingers on the strings and fretboard.

The image below provides a snapshot of the numberings and letterings of the fingers.

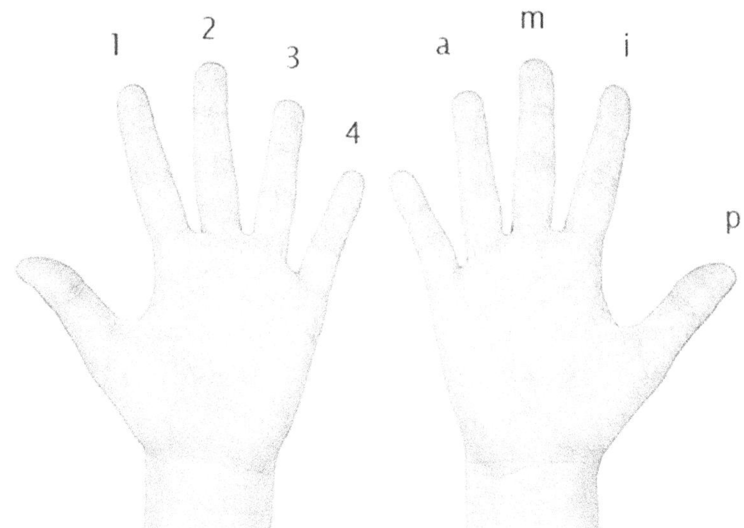

Finger Calluses

As you start to play, you will notice some pain on your fingertips, which later turns to a thick layer of dry skin. These are calluses. That is your body's natural way of numbing the pain that comes from continuous guitar practice. Normally, it takes between 2-4 weeks before the calluses develop, and the pain gives way. So what should you do to get over this as fast as you can?

- Take only short but frequent practice exercises every day.

- Start with the heavy strings first. Stop when you begin to feel pain and resume shortly after

- Keep your fingernails trimmed.

- Dry fingertips with alcohol

- Strum only with the thumb

Using a Pick

A very reliable and efficient alternative to using your thumb for playing is getting a plectrum, otherwise known as a guitar pick. A pick is a flat thick plastic device used for guitar picking. It can be used to strum chords or play individual notes. The importance of picks can be seen by the need to strike more distinct notes or play faster, especially while building your strumming techniques. Handling a pick essentially substitutes the need for the right index finger (i) and your thumb (p) because the pick is held between both of these. The ideal position for holding a pick is keeping it in-between the middle of your index finger and thumb. Beginners may find using a pick cumbersome, and if so, you may leave the pick at first, and learn how to play with your thumb. When you get comfortable using your thumb, then you return to the pick if you choose to.

Beginner Tips

At this point, you are now well aquatinted with the basics, but before we kick things off in the next chapter, keep the following tips in mind, as they will keep you in check and help you avoid common pitfalls made by many guitarists.

- Avoid the temptation to always tune your guitar

- Always take breaks in between practices

- Avoid the left hand "death grip," a situation where instead of pressing the strings with your fingertips, you press with the flat pad of your finger.

- Rehearse both in sitting and standing positions, for flexibility

- • Always stick to the correct fingering pattern. If you build up bad habits, it will be hard to correct.

- If you fail at something, keep up the practice. That's how you get to learn it.

- Make it fun! Enjoy yourself.

Chapter 2

Guitar Fretboard and Scales

Notes on the Fretboard

Do you know the single most important secret of any skilled guitar player? I believe you guessed right.

Yes, it is a thorough knowledge of the fretboard - theoretically and practically. Every single note you will ever play on your guitar is on the fretboard. Mastering the fretboard is the soloist's game-changer. Refer to the diagram below for a visual representation of the fretboard.

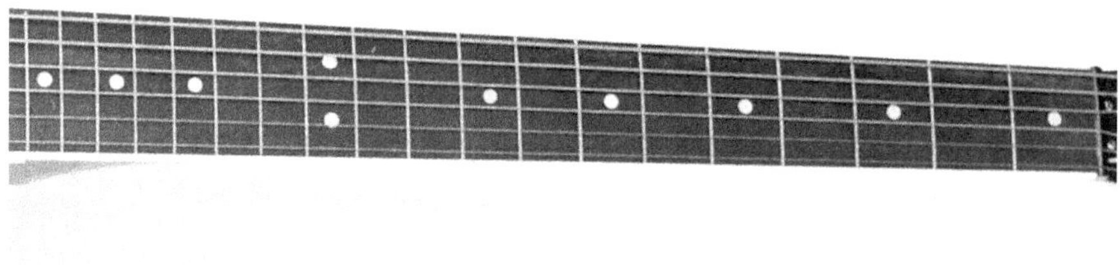

At this stage, we're not talking about memorizing the notes yet. You'll need to know them before committing them to memory. Also, the more practice you have, the easier it is to memorize the notes.

Fret Numbering

We begin with fret numbering. The 1st fret is the one just after the headstock. The second comes after the first, and so on down to the body of the guitar. Also, note that the fret numbers are the same on all the strings - from the 1st to the 6th.

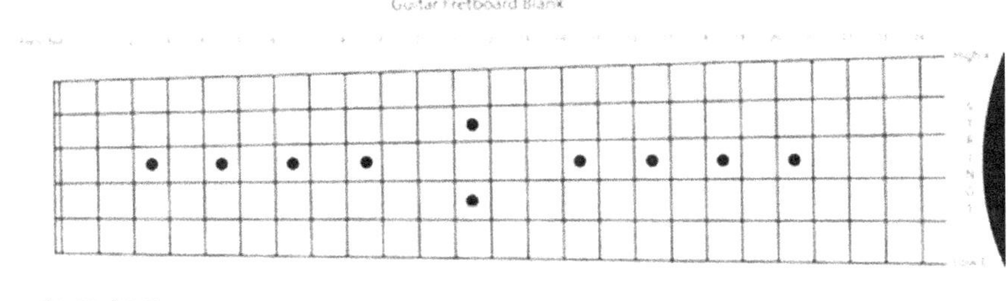

Always play behind the note you want to fret. So when fretting, place the fingertips on the string just behind the fret you want to play. For instance, the 5th fret is located between the 4th and 5th frets; the 3rd fret is located behind the 2nd and 3rd frets, and so on.

Next, when we talk about the zero fret on any string, we are simply referring to that string played 'open,' i.e., without holding the string down behind any fret. An open string is also known as an unfretted string - the natural note of that string is what is sounded.

Notes

Building on the knowledge from the previous section, we now have to identify the notes on the fretboard. In this case, we're not talking about the natural notes of the strings. Here, we're referring to the sounds that come out of the guitar whenever the strings are fretted behind any fret. Understanding guitar notes is highly essential because they are building blocks for all chords and solos. See the diagram below for the complete number of notes from the first to the 12th fret.

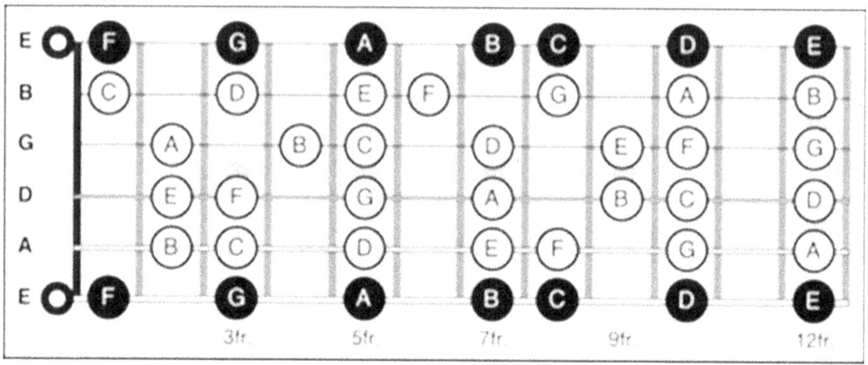

Also, note the natural notes of each string:

1st - E

2nd - B

3rd - G

4th - D

5th - A

6th - E

The first and last strings have the same natural notes, and similar fret notes on them. The dots on the fretboard serve as a simple navigation guide for the easy location of the frets and notes you want to play. Typically, you'll find them on the 3rd, 5th, 7th, 9th, 12th, and 15th frets.

Tips to Note

1. Now, your 1st left finger should go to the first fret, place the 2nd finger behind the 2nd fret, place the 3rd finger behind the 3rd fret, and finally let the 4th finger rest on the 4th fret. As you progress to further frets, move your fingers accordingly,

i.e., the 1st fingers go to the 5th fret, the 2nd to the 6th fret, the 3rd to the 7th fret, and the 4th to the 8th fret.

2. Do not let the thumb curl around the neck of the guitar. Instead, let it rest slightly at the back of the fretboard

3. The thumb is best placed behind the same fret the first finger is playing, regardless of the string.

4. For the right hand, two important strokes need to be noted: the downstroke, which is done with the thumb, and the rest stroke, which is played with the other three fingers. The rest stroke typically is an upward swing of the fingers, without moving the wrist.

The Cifra Notation

This is a simple form of tablature to represent musical notes on the fretboard. An open note is usually represented by a hollow circle on the string, while a fretted note is represented by a shaded circle. The Cifra system makes it easy to represent activities on the guitar in an easy to understand way. We'll be using this illustration method subsequently.

Guitar Scales

An essential ingredient in music theory or even guitar music scales. You must have heard people repeatedly make use of the word 'scales' on the guitar. That's because you really cannot do without learning these. In fact, all that you do with the guitar is segmented into scales. Guitar scales are ordered or organized sequences of notes played in ascending or descending order. That's it. Think of the individual notes you have to strike to create a short musical piece. The entire progression of notes played either in the ascending or descending order is known as a scale. In simpler words, a scale is any set of notes ordered by pitch. Guitarists use scales to create harmonies, melodies, and different musical arrangements. There are several scales on the guitar. On a keyboard, the complete chromatic scale is the collection of all the 7 white keys and the 5 black keys next to them. Those keys represent all the 12 notes in Western music. On the guitar, things are a little different. For example, all the scales would be notes starting from the open E note on the first string up to the open E note on the 6th string. The chromatic scale on the guitar is the 1st-4th frets beginning from the first to the last string. You may practice this on your guitar for better visualization. On the guitar, there are several types of scales, which we will discuss in detail soon.

First, to get a better understanding of scales, we need to understand a few other concepts, namely semitones, whole tones, intervals, keys, sharps, flats, and naturals.

Points to Note:

1. The scale must be arranged either in ascending or descending order within a given octave and then by repeating the same pattern in all octaves.

2. Scales are rudimentary in guitar music so that you can't create harmony or melody without them.

Half-Steps, Whole-Steps, and Intervals

On the guitar, there are individual notes or pitches, which are all denoted by the music alphabet:

A B C D E F G

So when you change a move from one note or pitch to another, it is called a change of pitch. A half-step is a change of pitch between a note and another note; one fret up or down. For example, if you move from the 4th fret on the 2nd string to the 5th fret of the same string, it is called a half-step. This difference in notes is known as a semitone. A whole-step, on the hand, is the movement from a note to another note, two frets up or down. For example, if you move your first finger from the 1st fret on the 1st string to the 3rd fret on the same string, then you have a whole-step or a whole tone. So, each fret means a semitone, while two frets mean a tone. Another way to visualize this concept is by using a keyboard. On the piano, then, a half-step is the distance between two consecutive white keys. But a whole-step is the distance between two keys, separated by a third key in-between them.

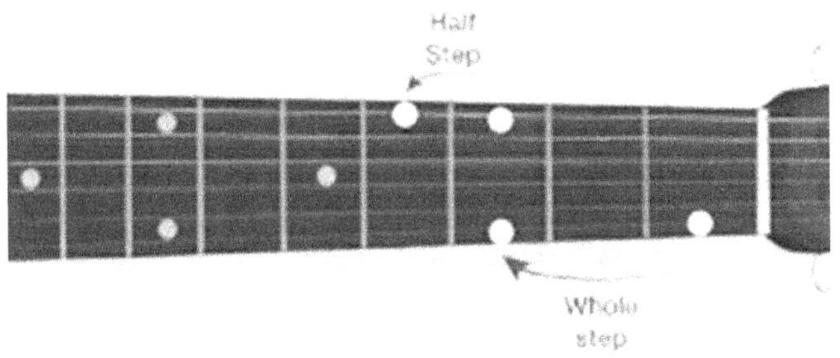

Now, on the guitar, let's say for situations where you move from the first fret to the 4th fret that will be called one and a half steps or simply an **interval,** which is made up of semi-tones (in this case 3 semitones or Half-Steps). These intervals can take up to 12 semitones, according to the number of frets on the fretboard. You may also see intervals as the gap between each note of the scale, with respect to the root note.

Keys

A key is normally related to a scale in an intricate manner. A scale is often named in accordance with the key that begins a scale. Hence, a scale is the root note or 'tonic' of any sequence of scales. So, any musical piece we create, going up or down, will be based on that particular key, with that key forming a part of the scale. For instance, if we play a scale consisting of 5 notes, say **E A B C E**, then that scale takes its root in the E key. We can call that scale an E scale.

Meanwhile, we should also bear in mind that every scale is essentially comprised of individual keys, starting with the root key or note. In the scale sited above, we have a scale made up of notes **E, A, B, C,** and **E,** where the root or tonic key is **E.** An understanding of keys is essential because once you know which key you're playing in; it becomes easy for you to switch pitches without messing things up. In summary, keys provide you with a root for your scales.

In the image below, we have an A major scale. Note how the scale begins and ends on the same notes. The notes do not have to be of the same pitch, but they have to sound alike.

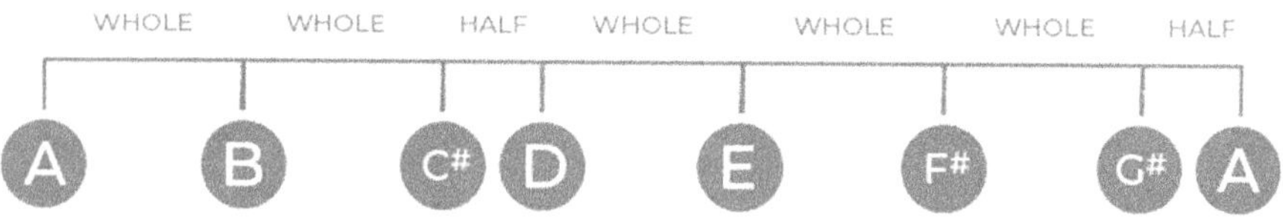

Sharps, Flats, and Naturals

Another essential, rudimentary concept in music generally is that of flats and sharps. They are mainly the half-step relatives of the seven major keys. A natural musical note is one that is sounded naturally without altering it. This can be any of the seven notes we already know. We can otherwise refer to them as **naturals.**

Sharps are one half-step increments in natural notes. They alter the natural notes by raising it by one semitone (denoted by #). **Flats**, on the other hand, do the exact opposite. It lowers natural notes by one semitone or a half-step (denoted by *b*). In summary, a sharp is one semitone higher in pitch, while a flat is one semitone lower. See the illustration below.

$$\text{Sharp} = \sharp$$
$$\text{Flat} = \flat$$
$$\text{Natural} = \natural$$

Guitar Scales Every Beginner Must Know

In guitar music, there are basically two types of scales - the major and minor scales. All other scales take their roots from these two. Other scales include the Dorian scale, Blue scale, Diatonic scale, pentatonic scales, and Mixolydian scale. So we'll walk through the major and minor scales, and then proceed to the rest. These two scales are very important in music.

The Major and Minor Scales

Let's use the C key for our illustration. The C key has no sharps or flats, so a C major scale would be:

C D E F G A B

On the guitar, we have it as:

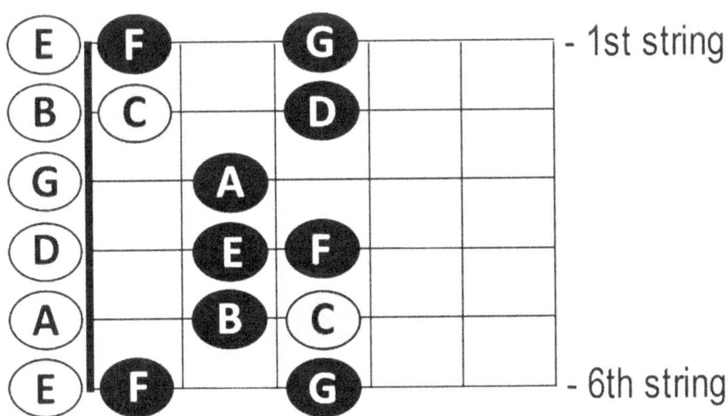

This is pretty straightforward because there are only natural notes in this scale, and it begins with the C key. The C minor scale takes a different turn instead. Since the C key is the tonic or root key, other notes or keys in that scale are, therefore, minor keys. For example, A minor scale begins with the A key instead. It is still a C scale but a C minor because it takes root from the A note, and all the other keys are the same.

A B C D E F G

The Chromatic Guitar Scales

The chromatic scale is the most basic of all scales in guitar music, in Western music in general. It consists of all the 12 notes in Western music, i.e., the 7 natural notes and 5 accidental notes (the shape and flats). Essentially, all other guitar scales are derived from the chromatic scale. Most guitarists do not play or use the chromatic scale. The reason for this is that all the melodies and harmonies you create are basically derivatives of the chromatic scale. So, the 12-note chromatic scale is not exactly interesting in itself; it only forms a basis for generating advanced scales. On the keyboard, the chromatic scale is the 7 white keys and the 5 black keys in-between them. To visualize this on the guitar, we play the open E on the sixth string up to the 12th fret (high E) on the same string. It is important to note that there are about 5 important scales which beginner guitarists should know:

- The major scale

- The natural minor scale

- The pentatonic scales

- The blue scale and

- The Dorian scale

Pentatonic Scales

Pentatonic scales are widely used, perhaps the most common of all guitar scales, especially in rock and pop music. Pentatonic scales are of two types – minor and major. As the name implies, there are only five (5) notes on any pentatonic scale. Remember, the major scales have 7 notes, so the pentatonic scale is just 2 notes less. They are the simplest scales and are a good place for beginners to start. The characteristic difference between the major scale and pentatonic scale is the absence of the 4th and 7th notes of the major scale in the pentatonic scale. As with all major and minor scales, there are formulae for major and minor pentatonic scales.

Formulae for major and minor pentatonic scales are shown here.

Pentatonic Scale	Scale Degrees
Minor	$1, 3_{flat,} 4, 5, 7_{flat}$
Major	$1, 2_{sharp}, 3, 4, 6_{sharp}$

Note: *the scale degrees represent the notes of a major scale*

Bearing in mind that the A major scale is comprised of A, B, C, D, E, F, G, and A, let's find the notes of the A minor pentatonic scale, using the formula, and this will be our result.

Pentatonic Scale	Scale Degrees
A Minor	A, C, D, E, G, and A
A Major	A, B, C#, E, F#, and A

Note the Difference:

- *A minor – removal of the 2ⁿᵈ and 6ᵗʰ notes, and flattening of the 3ʳᵈ and 7ᵗʰ notes.*

- *A major – removal of the 4ᵗʰ and 7ᵗʰ notes from the major scale.*

As opposed to blindly memorizing the platonic scale, you can see that it is easier to learn the formulae, and you are better grounded when you understand the theory.

To further solidify your understanding of pentatonic scales, let's consider some common practical examples.

1. **A Minor Pentatonic Scale (5ᵗʰ Position)**

This is a very common scale and is a fairly easy scale to develop your fret fingers.

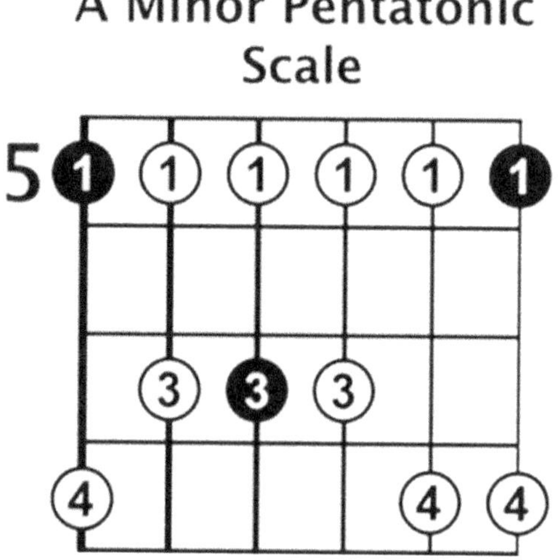

Now, to play this scale, on the low E string, i.e., the 6ᵗʰ string, place your 1ˢᵗ left finger on the 5ᵗʰ fret and then move the 4ᵗʰ finger to the 8ᵗʰ fret. This should be easy. Next, you go to the B string, and place your 1st finger still on the 5th fret, and your 3rd finger on the 7th fret. Once you've sounded the notes here, move to the 3rd or G string and then place your 1st and 3rd fingers on the 5th and 3rd frets, respectively. Notice that this is a repetitive pattern that should be repeated on the D string. On the A string, simply place your 1st finger on the 5th fret and 4th finger on the 8th fret. Repeat this for the high E string.

2. **A Major pentatonic Scale**

Here, according to the formula, the 4th and 7th notes are left out.

A Major Pentatonic Scale

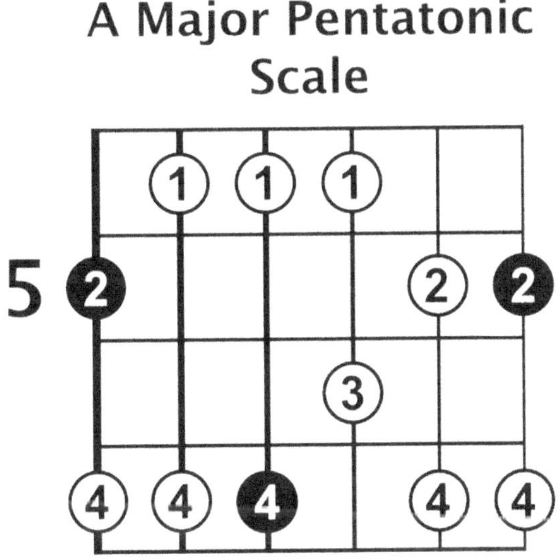

Following the pattern for playing the A Minor pentatonic scale, you can easily play this scale. It is important that you train your ears to master the sounds of each scale as you practice. That way, you also memorize the scales. Work your way slowly at first, and pick up the pace as you practice.

Other pentatonic scales include the G major pentatonic scale and E minor pentatonic scale.

The Natural Minor Scale

This is another essential must-know scale for beginners. It is not just foundational, but one that finds application in several country, contemporary rock, and blues tunes. In other words, it is widely used. Besides, it brings a somewhat opposite feel to the major scales. I think this scale gives you one of the best sounds you can ever get from your guitar scales. Sometimes, it is simply called the minor scale or Aeolian mode. It is heptatonic, i.e. it typically contains 7 notes. The difference between the minor scale and the major scale is that the 3rd, 6th, and 7th notes are flattened by one semitone each. They follow the interval pattern illustrated below:

W-H-W-W-H-W-W

Tips to Note:

1. *The black dots represent the root notes (which in this case is A)*

2. *W- whole step, H-half step*

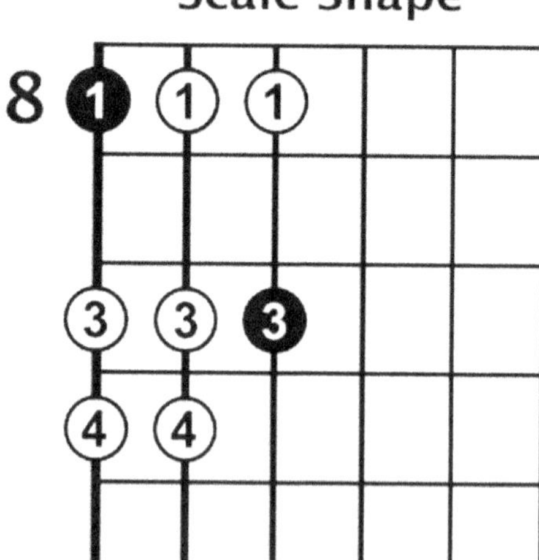

The Scale above is a C minor scale. As you can see, the fretting originates mainly from the 8th fret and includes the 10th and 11th frets. Do not bother about your dexterity yet. First, get comfortable with the shape and fretting the scale; the speed and dexterity will come as you practice.

Note that the minor scales are very similar to the major scales, except for the root key in each case. Remember, the root key is the alternative starting note for playing a major scale. Therefore, changing the root key of any scale means changing the key of the entire scale. So, in the example we cited above, the C minor scale is.

A B C D E F G

Minor scales could be Natural Minor Scales, Harmonic Minor Scales, or the Melodic Minor Scales. Mostly, when people talk about minor scales, they are referring to the natural minor scales.

The Major Scale (5th Position)

This is one of the most important scales you should know and memorize. For guitarists aspiring to be pros, you just can't do without this scale. It is as important as it is fundamental in your mastery of the guitar. The major scale is a heptatonic scale, which means it has 7 notes and a pattern or formula of:

W W H W W W H

When we use this formula to derive an A major scale, what we'll get is:

A B C D E F G A

Since the 3rd and last notes are semitones (half-steps), we have to flatten them:

A B C# D E F G# A

To play this scale, we will have the shape illustrated below:

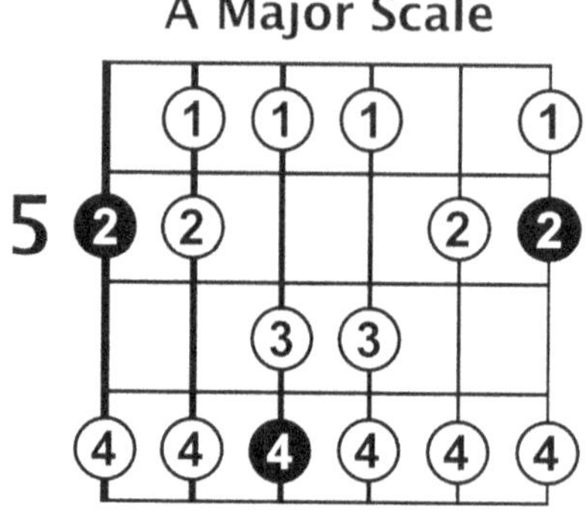

Remember, the number outside the box indicates the fret number, while the numbers on the strings indicate your fingers accordingly. Gradually master the shape of the scale before getting creative.

The Blue Scale

This scale is a six-note scale (hexatonic) and has a step pattern of **W – W – H – H – W – W**. It is very similar to the Minor Pentatonic Scale. The difference is just in the addition of one note to the scale, the flat 5 note. The Blues scale gives a great sound that makes it common among blues, country, and rock guitarists, and you'll hear it when you play it! There are several blues scale shapes. As an example, the E Blues scale is provided for practice here. It is easier to master the rest once you're comfortable with one.

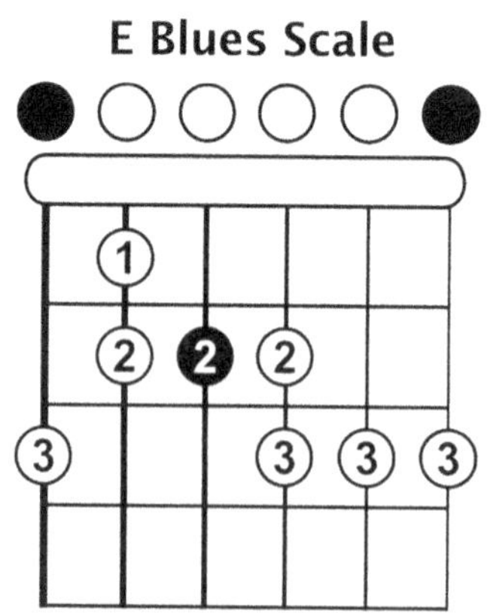

In this case, you start from the 1st fret to the 3rd fret. Compared with the minor pentatonic scale, everything else is the same, aside from the additional flat 5 note.

The Dorian Scale

This scale is the second mode of the G major scale (i.e., it is heptatonic), with a formula of W H W W W H W. It is particularly used for playing over an unrelated minor scale. The Dorian mode is a minor scale which has a b3 (i.e., the 3rd note of the major scale is taken half-step down), and is commonly used in jazz and blues music. A typical example is the D Major scale: D E F# G A B C# D. You'll notice that the 3rd and 7th notes have been lowered by one half-step each.

Tips for Effective Scale Practice

1. When playing scales, look out for patterns within the scale shapes. This will help you memorize them.

2. Master the shape of the scales before spicing them up

3. Take note of the root notes or tonic keys

4. Start slowly and progress to mastery of each scale before moving to another

5. You have to understand the basic scale patterns and formula

6. You DON'T need to know ALL the scales; even professional guitarists don't. Only master a few and learn as you grow.

7. Be sure to use the tip of your finger for fretting; otherwise, you'll produce dull sounds.

8. As with regular guitar practice, commit considerable time toward mastering the scales but rest once you are tired, and resume later.

9. Stick to correct fingerings as you practice.

Intervals

As a guitarist, your ultimate goal will be to gain full mastery of the fretboard. Remember, I said earlier that everything you'll ever play as a guitarist is on the fretboard. In this section, let's focus on the fretboard a little more, and elaborate on the concept of intervals. The importance of intervals in guitar music is closely tied to your grasp of scales and chords. In fact, intervals are the building blocks of music – not just guitar music. Moreover, developing the ability to improvise is dependent on understanding intervals. Let's get to it already!

As we already established at the beginning of the chapter, an interval is a distance between the root note on any scale or chord and another note on that scale or chord. Imagine you want to play a G major scale; the root note on that scale is G, an interval is a distance from that note to any other note on the G major scale. On the fretboard, an interval is basically the distance between any two notes or pitches. Recall that fretboard notes can be either a half-step (semitone) or whole-step (whole-tone) apart, and one fret is a semitone, while two frets make a whole tone. So, an interval could be just one semitone or several whole tones.

Using our G major scale example, the chromatic scale would be:

G, G# or Ab, A, A# or Bb, B, C, C# or Db, D, D# or Eb, E, F, F# or Gb

This might seem confusing, but remember there are 12 notes in the chromatic scale; 7 natural notes (A, B, C, D, E, F, and G) and 5 sharps/flats notes. Keep in mind that when we use a flat (b), it means a fret lower, i.e., a semitone, and a sharp (#) means a whole tone (two semitones). Another important point to note is that intervals are numbered with figures. So, in the example above, we can say that there are 12 intervals, with each note representing an interval. Taking a five-note interval to say, A - E, for example, we can play this interval at different pitches across the fretboard, depending on where we start. The same applies to different intervals. Now, each interval has a name, meaning that there are different types of intervals on the guitar. But before we consider that, let's discuss the two ways intervals can be played.

Melodic Intervals

When you play all the notes in a scale one at a time, you have a melodic interval. Regardless of whether the notes are played on the same or different strings, up or down the fretboard, or whether it contains just two or more tones, as long as the notes are played individually, it is a melodic interval. A practical example is when you're soloing.

Harmonic Interval

When the notes are played vertically, all at the same time, then you have a harmonic interval, i.e., the notes all blend into one harmony. A practical example of this is when you're strumming a chord.

In summary, we can assert that melodic intervals are the building blocks of scales, while harmonic intervals are the building blocks of chords and chord progressions.

Names and Structure of Intervals

While it's okay to use your ears to identify intervals, naming intervals serves two purposes: for easier identification and communication among musicians. Using the G major scale we highlighted above, you'll see that the root note is G, also known as the first-degree interval. Going further along the scale, the second-degree note is called the major 2nd interval, and the third degree is called the major 3rd interval, the fourth and fifth are the perfect 4th and the perfect 5th, while the sixth and seventh degrees are called major 6th and major 7th. So these interval numbers, 1-7 represent the exact positions of the notes, while the degree tells us the specific number of notes in the scale. For example, if we remove the 2nd and 6th intervals from the G major scale, we have 5 notes left, making the new scale a 5 note or 5 degrees scale (that's a pentatonic scale if you remember). The structure of the new scale is 1, 3, 4, 5, and 7 notes, i.e., G, B, C, D, F. Same number of intervals but different tones.

Having this clarity on intervals and scales will simplify things for you and make you more flexible on the fretboard.

Types of Intervals

Being that each interval has a name and definite position when we alter these positions by moving the notes one free down or one fret up, we obtain different sounds, other than the natural notes in the G Major scale. These different sounds give rise to the varying types of intervals (beginning from the root note up to one octave), as we will see below.

Perfect Unison

If, for instance, you play the notes from the open G string to the open higher E string in unison, with a single stroke, then you'll have a harmonic interval. The sound produced is a nice harmony of all the strings; the interval between them is technically zero because the strings are open. This is also a good way to check if your guitar is in tune.

Minor Second Interval

Consider, the Gmaj chromatography scale again. If we dropped the position of the 2nd-degree note by a fret, i.e., if it becomes b2, we'll have Ab. The interval was a major second interval, but it is now a minor second interval. Note that this is the smallest Interval on the fretboard because it's just one fret or one semitone lower than the natural note. Remember, the root note is G. When you play the harmonic Interval of the scale, notice the dissonance in the sound, though the melodic Interval might sound just fine. Alternatively, this interval can be called m2 interval.

Major Second Interval

Let's say that we are back on the second degree's natural position, which is one fret or a semitone higher than the minor second interval. This time, we'll have a major second or M2 interval.

The sound is a bit unstable still but clearly different from the previous one.

Tip to note: In naming intervals, m is used to represent minor intervals while M is used for Major Intervals.

Minor Third Interval

So if the 3rd interval has dropped a semitone lower than the major 3rd interval, the new position gives rise to a minor 3rd interval. When played together with the other intervals, we get a much better sound called a consonance. This is an important characteristic feature of minor scales and chords. You can see this new position as a whole tone and a half in relation to that of the root note.

Major Third Interval

The same applies here as in the major second. The minor third interval has moved a fret or one semitone upward to give a third major interval or M3, which gives Major chords and scales a bright and harmonious quality. Note that this the same as the natural position of the 3rd-degree note.

Perfect 4th Interval

If you try to move the 4th note a semitone lower, you'll notice we can't because the 3rd is just at that same position. So, we can only move it higher by a semitone or a fret. This creates a perfect 4th interval, which is two and a half whole tones away, relative to the root note of the scale. Alternatively, we call this a P4 interval or augmented 4th. If you look at this again, you'll see that we've only sharpened the 4th note by taking it a fret higher - the same thing as bringing the 4th note a fret lower. In relation to the root note, the augmented or perfect 4th is three whole tones away. As with the others, when you play the new scale, the sound is unique. Always take note of the positions and sounds of each scale.

Diminished 5th

This is exactly the same as the augmented 4th because the interval is just one fret below the 5th note, i.e., a flat 5. What then is the difference? The augmented 4th is used when a 5th note is present. But when a 4th note is present instead of a scale, the diminished 5th is used. When two different intervals share similar pitches like this, they're called enharmonic intervals. The presence of other intervals determines which is to be used.

Perfect 5th (Minor 6th)

As you can guess, we obtain this interval by flattening the 6th interval. That gives us a sharp 5, an augmented 5th, or a minor 6th. It is positioned three whole tones and one semitone in relation to the root note of the scale. This is the same as moving one fret or semitone higher than the perfect 4th interval. The P5 Interval is an essential one for guitarists. We'll find out more about this in chapter four.

However, according to the rule we establish for enharmonic intervals, if the 5th note is present, we revert to using the minor sixth (m6). It is practically the same position as the perfect fifth. Hence, in this case, the interval played is a minor 6th.

Major Sixth Interval

Following the same formula, the major 6th is one fret or semitone higher than the minor 6th interval and is pretty much the same position as the natural 6tg degree note. For our Major G scale, the practical note here will be the F note. Note the difference between this interval and the minor 6th - in sound and visualization.

Minor 7th Interval

This is as easy as the others before it. We simply move the major 6th one fret or one semitone up, i.e., a sharp 6 or flat 7th (also diminished 7th).

An m7 Interval is usually a whole tone lower than the root note on the fretboard. It is practically found in Mixolydian scales. Notice that the sound is somewhat dissonant and unstable.

Major Seventh

This is just one fret or a semitone lower than the root note, and also one fret higher than the minor 7th Interval. It is the last note on the chromatic scale, just before the octave is reached.

The octave is the beginning of a higher pitch or interval altogether. It is a natural 8th note in relation to the root note. Octaves are particularly used in power chords. This is because it is an interval with a perfect consonant sound. You'll find the importance and further applications of intervals in the shapes of scales and the construction of chords later. One particular practical function of intervals is that it shows us the difference between minor and major scales and chords. Irrespective of the root node, if any scale, the intervals follow the same rule. A minor 7th scale, for example, will have the following structure:

1 2 ♭3 4 5 ♭6 ♭7

W W H W W H H

Intervals, therefore, allow for better visualization of scales and chords on the fretboard. This rule follows for all kinds of scales and intervals. I also suggest that you spend time practicing the shapes and sounds of each interval as a trained ear is an asset every musician should have.

Tip to Note:

1. Intervals are relative regardless of where they're played on the fretboard, i.e., whether the root note is A or G, the relationship between the root notes and other notes remains the same.

2. These relationships are movable, i.e., they can be moved to anywhere on the fretboard. The only thing that changes is the pitches produced.

What Every Guitarist Must Know

In the art of gaining mastery of the guitar, there are tricks, shortcuts, cheats, and enduring practices. Every guitarist soon has to work out and stick to what and which works best for them, depending on what they aim to achieve, after picking up the guitar. As an example, you'll find that there are many cheats and shortcuts to learning guitar scales. I am not saying that those are bad in themselves because, in the end, some will give you the results you want.

But, the ideal thing would be to first understand the basics and theory behind them. That way, it becomes easier for you to improvise and create your own style - even with the shortcuts. As a matter of fact, getting your own sound will later become one of your most valued assets as a guitarist. You don't want to always sound like your teacher, even though it's essential to have a teacher. The point really is, your creativity is what makes the whole mix entertaining. Learning to play isn't enough to make you a pro; perhaps it is just enough to get you going. But if you want to be more than just a regular guitar player, you've got to also learn some rudimentary theories, and that leads us to the next section.

Does A Guitarist Need To Understand Music Theory?

This is a tricky question, but yes, you need to. The popular opinion seems to favor the opposite because it's less stressful. However, you don't have to study all the jargon in music theory to become a star guitarist. You could really sound good with little or without any knowledge of music theory. But a lack of theoretical knowledge can be a very big disadvantage to you as well. A good grasp of the basics and a few more hooks can help you create irresistible licks with your guitar.

For example, being able to understand theory will help you improve your techniques to produce a refined sound. You'll be doing yourself a lot of good by understanding music, at least enough to support your skills. Think of it this way; do you prefer to learn a language by studying and speaking it or just by speaking it? The language of music is rooted in theory behind it. There are two important strokes to guitar music mastery: training your ears and understanding what you are playing. The two go hand in hand. Ultimately, with a good ear, you will be able to create the best kind of sound when you are capable of approaching things with a piece of theoretical knowledge.

Chapter 3

Chords and Chord Progression

Understanding Chords

The subject of chords in guitar music is vast, and so are the techniques involved. Most beginners find it overwhelming, which is why you won't find a lot of guitarists who have an in-depth understanding of chord structure. The need to quickly learn and memorize as many as possible could lead beginners to make mistakes. Also, one needs to be sure of which to start with and which to progress to. However, there's an approach that works. Understanding the theory of chords helps you to improve your music in ways that benefit you in the long run. With a sound grounding in chord construction, you can even write your own songs. In essence, it is not enough to know how to play; it is best when you understand what makes up the sounds you produce from your guitar. And the good part is that you can work your way up, one step at a time. In this chapter, we'll work through the important basics, and then we'll look at some advanced stuff, especially the things you need the most. Note that you will need to understand the fretboard and scales for a better understanding of chords.

Guitar chords are sets of notes (3 - 4 in most instances) played together and simultaneously. They can also be played sequentially in an arpeggio. In other words, chords require the ability to use your fretting fingers smartly. There are several types of chords - for simple and sophisticated songs. As we proceed, you'll see how chords are connected to scales and intervals, which we learned in the preceding chapter.

Chords Theory and Construction

As mentioned earlier, chords are made up of three or more different notes played together. Take, for example, the G major chord, which is composed of the B, D, and G notes. These notes are the components of the G major chord. Like many other chords, it can be played in more than one shape, meaning that you move to other frets to play a higher or lower-pitched version of the same chord. It is also important to bear in mind that these notes are also referred to as intervals when it comes to chord construction.

In this case, the G note is the root note and the first interval, while the B and D notes are the 3rd and 5th intervals. Hence, the intervals that make up the G major chord are 1, 3, and 5. Subsequently, we'll discuss the different kinds of chords in guitar music.

Recall that:

1. The space between two notes on the fretboard is an interval

2. The space between two consecutive notes is a half-step

3. The space between two notes separated by a third note is a whole-step

4. An interval consists of a half-step to many whole-steps

Major Triads

These are chords made of 3 notes. These notes together are known as triads. Triads are major chords and constitute a majority of common chords used by guitarists. In terms of intervals, triads basically consist of 3 intervals. Triads could be major, minor, suspended, diminished, and augmented.

Major triads typically consist of the root note (1), the 3rd degree (3), and 5th degree (5) notes. These notes constitute the major chords on the major scale. Again, the root note gives the chord its name. So a major triad chord whose root note is A will be called an A major chord. A-C major chord, for example, begins with the C note, the 3rd and 5th notes are B and E notes respectively. So when fretting this chord, your fingers will rest on only these three notes. Meanwhile, the open strings have the same notes as the triad notes. This applies to all major chords. Notice that the fingering is done in such a way that captures the 1 3 5 positions for the constituent notes.

Minor Triads

These are chords that also contain 3 notes. Every other detail remains the same except in the 3rd-degree note (the 2nd interval in the chord). The difference is only in the 3rd note, i.e., the Minor triad chords consist of the root note (1), the minor 3rd note (flattened), and the 5th-degree note (5). Now, referring to the example we used in the major chord category, we can convert the C major chord to C minor chord by dropping the B note a semitone lower than it is in the major chord. So we have **C ♭B E.**

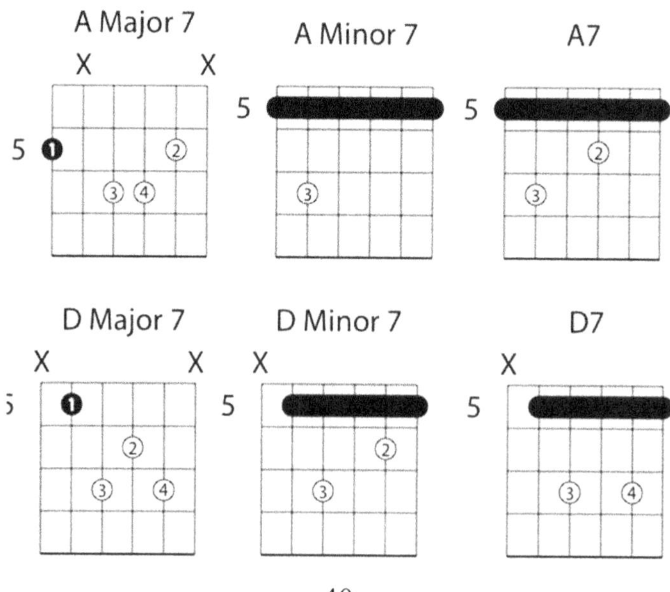

So, in fretting a minor triad chord, we use a flattened 3rd-degree note (i.e., moving one fret down) to sound the chord. See illustration below:

Suspended Chords

These are also three-note chords. As the name suggests, these use three chords. Suspended chords (sus) are neither minor nor major chords since the characteristic 3rd-degree note is absent. It's replaced by the perfect 4th interval instead. The 4th note lies at a position one semitone above the regular 3rd note. A suspended 4th chord is written as **1 4 5**.

If the chord we're looking at is an A chord (with its root note as A), then we write it as Asus4. If it is B, we say it is Bsus4, and so on. The most important thing about fretting suspended chords is paying attention to the 2nd interval (4th note). Ignore the 3rd-degree note we have in the regular major and minor chords, place your finger on the 4th fret instead, which is one semitone higher than the 3rd note on the major scale. For example, the component notes of the Asus4 chord are **A** (1st) **C** (4th) **E** (5th). Notice that the 4th note is just one semitone higher.

A suspended chord can also be a suspended 2nd chord. The difference this time is the replacement of the 3rd chord with a 2nd chord. So we have it as **1 2 5**. Examples include Asus2, Bsus2, and Csus2. Using a C major chord, compare the difference in sounds between a Csus4 chord and the C major or C minor equivalents.

Augmented Chords

Augmented Chords are also triad chords, and are very similar to the major chords. The major difference is that the 5th-degree note is raised one semitone higher, i.e., it is a sharp note instead. Instead of having **1 3 5** as we see in the major chord scale, we have it as **1 3 #5** on the augmented chords.

When playing augmented chords, the important point to remember is that augmented chords have a sharpened 5th-degree note, regardless of the fretboard position you choose to use.

Diminished Chords

This is a triad chord as well. It bears a resemblance to the minor chord in that it also has a flattened 3rd-degree note, but the difference here is it has a flattened 5th note as well. This is the configuration of a diminished chord:

1 $\flat$3 $\flat$5

Note that a major or minor scale could be played over both the augmented and diminished chords because of the sheer flexibility in fingering these chords.

7th Chords

In the previous section, we discussed the 5 triad chords. Since you're familiar with the triads, it will be much easier to understand the 7th major chords. The 7th chords are 4 notes chords, an extension of the major triads. Essentially, the 4th note is a 7th-degree note, hence their name. Just like their triad counterparts, they have several types.

Major 7th chords (Maj7)

Major 7th chords are simply an extension of the Major triads. They have a 7th-degree note in addition to the 3 notes in the corresponding major chord, the root note (1), the 3rd-degree note (3), the 5th-degree note (5th), and the 7th-degree note (7). This forms a major 7th chord. This chord is abbreviated Maj7. For example, if the chord has a C root, it'll be called the Cmaj7 chord. When playing the chord, you may experience difficulty getting all the notes under your fingers. In such situations, you may do without the less important notes and replace them with improvised ones as long as you have an understanding of what the scale is.

Dominant 7 Chords

In this category, the 7th-degree note (7) is flattened. Otherwise, every detail is the same as the 7th major chord.

1 3 5 ♭7

The dominant 7 chords are abbreviated by writing the root note together with 7. Hence, if we have a dominant 7 chord rooted in G, we simply say it's a G7 chord.

Minor 7th chords

Remember, when we earlier discussed minor chords, we maintained that the differentiating feature is the flattened 3rd-degree note. So, in this category, we simply make the 3rd and 7th notes flat to achieve a minor 7th chord sequence.

1 ♭3 5 ♭7

Note that as I said earlier, when playing, allow for some flexibility where you cannot finger all the notes on the chord. The beauty of it all is understanding the basic concepts behind the chords and applying them creatively by creating great sounds. The important aspect is sticking to the standard intervals.

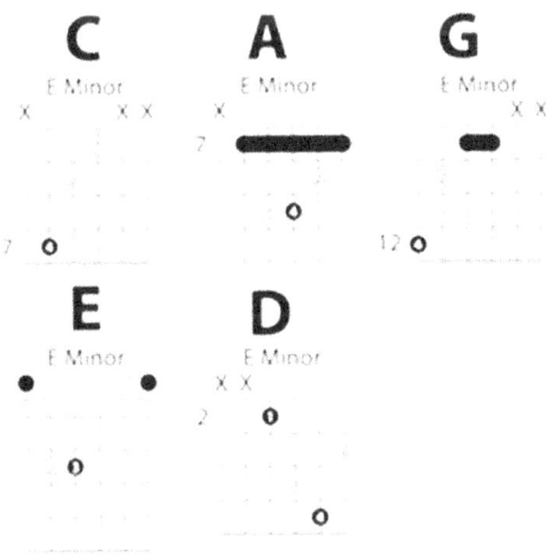

Augmented 7th Chords

The progression remains the same, compared to the augmented triads, except that the 7th note is flattened. 1 3 ♯5 ♭7

At this point, it will be getting increasingly difficult to hold down the notes of the augmented 7th chord. The feel of the chord is naturally tense, and it is used a lot in playing jazz music. When abbreviated, the augmented 7th chords are written as "aug7". Therefore, an augmented 7th major chord with root note B will be written as Baug7. The same applies to all other notes.

Half Diminished Chords

In this 7th chord, every component note is flattened except for the root note (1). As we've established already from the preceding categories, a typical 7th chord is formed by adding a 7th-degree note to the corresponding triad chord. Recall that the diminished triad chord has a root note and a flattened 3rd and 5th note. The half-diminished chords, therefore, includes an extra flat 7th note.

1 ♭3 ♭5 ♭7

In all, the 7th chords are much easier to understand and remember when you have a good understanding of the triads. Another way to remember this particular chord is seeing it as a minor 7th chord with a flat 5th.

Diminished 7th Chords

The diminished 7th chords are similar to the half-diminished 7th chords, but they have a double flattened 7th-degree note. This is an abbreviated dim7" example are Gdim7, Cdim7, etc.

1 ♭3 ♭5 ♭ ♭7

For remembrance, you can easily think of the diminished 7th chord as a minor triad chord with a flat 5th note and a double flat 7th note.

The diminished 7th chord has an interesting sound and is popular among guitarists.

Suspended 7th Chords

Think of a suspended triad chord (either sus4 or sus2) that has been extended by adding a flattened 7th-degree note. The distinguishing feature is, of course, the addition of a flat 7th (b7) note and introduction of either a 2nd or 4th note.

1 4 5 ♭ 7 - 7th suspended 4th chord

1 2 5 ♭ 7 - 7th suspended 2nd chord

If we have a 7th suspended 4th chord, which takes root in a C note, we write it as C7sus4. Other examples are B7sus4, G7sus2, etc.

The triads and 7th chords are basic chords that you'll need to understand. These two constitute up to 80% of what you'll see when it comes to common guitar chords. By now, you must be familiar with all the essential chords in these two categories. There are more complex chord constructions. But before you move on to those, I suggest you take some more time to study and familiarize yourself with chord shapes we have already discussed.

Chord Extensions

Now we know that the basic chords are the triads (3 notes) and 7th chords (4 notes). There are, in fact, more chords with 4 notes, and other advanced chords, which have more notes. These chords are called extended chords and are used to create fuller chords that produce richer harmonies and sweeter sounds. They typically extend up to the 9th, 11th, and 13th notes. Extended chords find particular application in jazz music, which is why they are called "jazz chords." Here, we'll see how to build these complex chord constructions.

First, let's look at how these chords are derived, and then we'll look at them individually. Consider the C major Octave below:

C D E F G A B C D

1 2 3 4 5 6 7 8 9

You'll notice that after the first octave, we begin again at key C, which is the keynote. This counting makes the D key the night note. Practically, the next C is at a higher octave or pitch, and so are the notes after it. Effectively, we can resume the counting from 1 instead of starting with 8, thereby making the 9th note the 2nd and so on.

C D E F G A B

9 10 11 12 13 14 15

So, we summarize these higher notes as:

- 9th (one octave plus a 2nd)

- 11th (one octave plus a perfect 4th)

- 13th (one octave plus a major 6th)

This is called fine stacking. These lower numbers represent the notes coming next in the chord scale, while the higher numbers simply mean the exact positions of the note or tone in sequential order (i.e., if you started counting from the very first octave). So, if our root tone is a C key, as shown above, the 9th tone will be the D key, which is actually the 2nd tone in that octave. I hope that is clear enough. Now, with this understanding, and keeping in mind the triads and 7th chords, we can delve into the chord structure for extended chords.

9th Chords

As explained earlier, these are chords that have 5 notes. In addition to the root note, they have the 3rd, 5th, 7th, and 9th tones. Like the other categories we discussed in the triads and 7th chords, 9th chords have different types as well. The major chords categories here are the major 9th, minor 9th, and the dominant 9th.

Major 9th

Abbreviated as Gmaj9, these chords are stacked up to the 9th note, and are composed of 5 natural notes:

1 3 5 7 9

When fingering these chords, remembering that the 9th note of the scale is the same as the 2nd, will help you improvise if necessary. Be mindful also that you may not be able to fret all the notes, depending on the strings you choose. In such a case, you may leave out the 5th note, and still retain the harmony of the chord.

Dominant 9th

Here we also have a pentatonic chord (5 notes), but the 7th is flattened, thereby making it a dominant 9th chord. This is written as C7 when the root note is a C key.

1 3 5 ♭7 9

Practically, we have this as C E G ♭ B D for the key C. Therefore; these are the notes; you'll get under your fingers when fretting this chord on the fretboard.

Minor 9th

This is abbreviated as m9 and written fully as Cm9, Gm9, and Em9, etc. Since it is a minor chord, remember, we'll have to flatten the 3rd-degree note. So we have it as:

1 ♭3 5 ♭7 9

The minor 9th chords are typically minor 7th chords extended by an additional 9th note.

11th Chords

Eleventh chords are 9th chords, which are extended to the 11th degree. They are rarely used or encountered in jazz music. However, the most common 11th chords are the suspended and minor 11ths, for example, C11sus4 (11th suspended 4th) and Cm11 (minor 11th). These are denoted as:

1 2 5 7 9 11 - suspended 11th chord

1 ♭3 5 7 9 11 - Minor 11th chords

You'll notice that what we have in chord theory at this point is almost practically impossible without a few compromises. So, I suggest leaving out the notes you can do without, but understand the intervals and basic chord shapes. You'll need that to be able to improvise when the need arises.

13th Chords

The 13th chords follow the same rule of extension. We simply add a 13th-degree note to the corresponding 11th chords to form a 13th chord (which composed of 6 noted). Note that the 13th chords are the highest possible chords in guitar chords. The may not necessarily include the 9th or 13th chord when being played. This is usually because of the dissonance produced, as one of the notes will be unharmonious with the rest. Besides, it is difficult to fret or sound all the 6 notes at the same time.

Major 13th

Major 13th chords are built by adding the 13th degree to the corresponding major 11th chord. As before, this is written as Cmaj13, for example. The major typically indicates that the 7th note is a major 7th.

1 3 5 7 9 11 13

Remember, the 9th and 11th notes can be left out of the scale, and the chord will still have its natural sound.

Minor 13th

The same procedure obtains here, except that the 3rd and 7th notes are flat (to make it a minor chord). Always refer to the triads and 7th chords for clarity, if it gets fuzzy at any point.

1 ♭3 5 ♭7 9 11 13

Examples for this category are Cm13, Gm13 and Am13.

Dominant 13th

The dominant 13th chord is neither a minor nor a major chord. So it has a flattened 7th-degree note as in the others (7th, 9th, and 11th) to indicate a dominant chord, written as A13, without the chord name.

1 3 5 ♭7 9 11 13

Added Chords

These are special chord progressions obtained from the omission of the 7th note. They contain chords up to the 13th notes, but without the 7th note in any chord. They are called added tone chords or simply add chords. The added tone refers to the notes that come after the missing 7th note.

For example, in an added 9th chord, using Aadd9 as reference (with A as root note), we have only 4 notes instead of 5:

1 3 5 9

This simple formula equally applies to the 11th and 13th chords structures.

1 3 5 13 or 1 3 5 11

When naming, we simply write the root note and include numbers 9, 11, or 13 after the word "add," e.g., Aadd13, Gadd9.

Tips to Note:

1. Before playing, be sure you understand the fretboard and the chord shape you want to play

2. Leave out the 5th note or other less important notes, if the fingering does not accommodate it.

3. Do not rush through the process. Take enough time to understand each chord and its shape before moving to the next.

4. Each chord structure is named after the last note. For example, the 9th chords are named after the 9th note.

5. When playing the 13th chords, the 11th notes are usually left out.

Chord Progressions

This is one of the most important things you'll need as a guitarist. Chord progressions can be described as a series of guitar chords played in a particular sequence on a scale. They usually consist of 2, 3, or 4 chords. At first, chord progressions will seem difficult, especially to play them smoothly. But with steady and focused practice, you'll get the hang of it. Before long, you'll be able to write your own songs. There are a number of common and easy progressions, to begin with. In this section, we'll work through a few of them. But ultimately, you'll need to build your dexterity on other chords.

Three Chord Progression

There are at least 3 different basic chord progressions under this category to get you started. We begin with the I IV V (1 4 5) progression. These chords can be used to play many songs. A typical example is the G-C-D chord progression, which has G major key as its root note. This means that all the chords are major chords. Note the changes as well. Take it slowly and pick up the pace later.

Note that these are open chords and are about the simplest chords you can begin with. Alternatively, you may start with the A E D major chords. Here, you can get creative; play the three chords interchangeably; play two before playing the third, and so on.

Next is the I ii V (1 2 5) progression. An example is the D Maj - Em7 - A7 progression. A popular method for playing this is in the 2 5 1 sequence. Note that the 2nd chord is a minor chord, which introduces a soft feel to the progression.

Note:

1. The Roman numerals indicate the scale degrees of the chords; those in uppercase indicate major chords, while the lower case means minor chords.

2. The strings marked "X" are not to be played

Four Chord Progression

This is another popular chord progression used in both old and contemporary music. A typical example is the I V VI IV (1 5 6 4) progression. So, in addition to the first three chords used in the first example above, a fourth chord (the 6 chord) is introduced to the mix. An important point to note is that the 6 chord is will be a minor chord because of its position. An E minor chord may be used here.

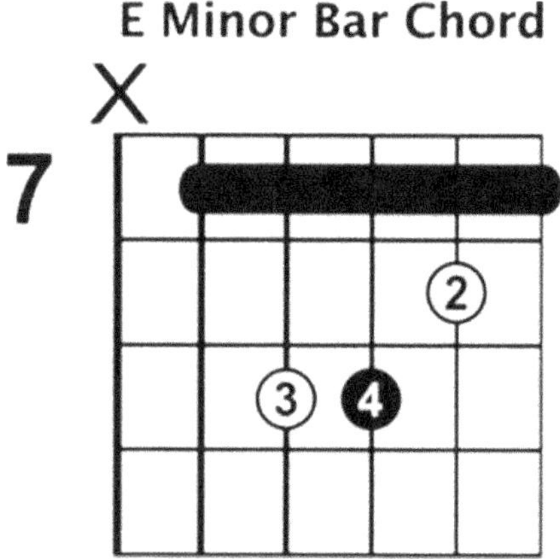

Tips to Note:

In chord progression, the 1st, 4th, and 5th positions are major chords.

The 2nd, 3rd, and 6th are minor chords.

Some other popular chord progressions are:

1. Diatonic chords- I-V (C-G).

2. I –vi-IV-V (D-Em-F-G)

3. I-ii-V (C-Am-G)

4. I-IV-V (A-E-D)

5. I-vi (C-Am)

CAGED Guitar System

You must have noticed that you can only do so much on the fretboard with just four fingers. A practical example is when we discussed extended chords, we had to leave out some less important notes in the chord scale. We had to leave out the root notes in some cases, and in others, we sacrificed the 5th or 11th-degree notes, so we could focus on the notes that gave the best sounds for each chord. So, as we stack up notes and build extended or richer chord voicing, it becomes increasingly difficult to finger all of the notes on the fretboard. Well, there's a way around this challenge. Guitarists use a method called the CAGED system to beat the issue of insufficient fingers. It is based on the open chords of five major chords: C, A, G, E, and D chords. We will see in the subsequent paragraphs, how the CAGED system can be leveraged to build richer guitar voicing.

Bar Chords

If you look closely, you'll notice that these chords are open chords, i.e., they have open notes or strings in their chord scales (identifiable by the hollow circles on top of the charts). Now, these chord arrangements are moveable, which means, for example, that you can play the C major chord in the A chord shape. See the illustration below.

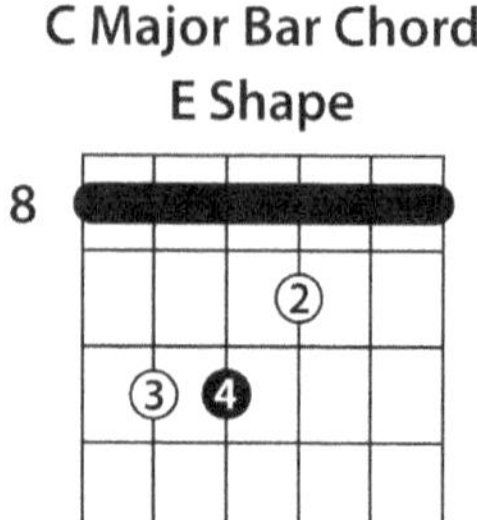

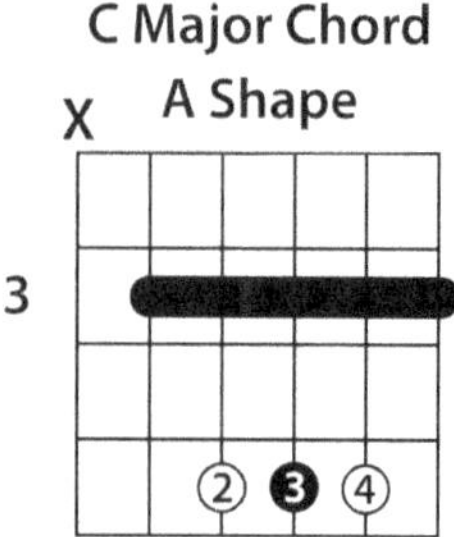

C Major Chord

The same technique applies to every other chief shape, and that's what the CAGED system is based on. We'll examine each of them at a time, starting with the C major chord. The idea here is basically to bar the open notes by adjusting the positions of the fingers on the fretboard while still maintaining a harmonious sound on the guitar. The CAGED system finds vast application in advanced chord voicing, playing arpeggios (we will discuss this in detail later on), and learning chords and scales.

The C Shape

The C major chord is the first in the series and will form the basis for the adjustments in the other chords. Remember, it is an open chord. The purpose is to play the shape if the successive chords to play the preceding ones.

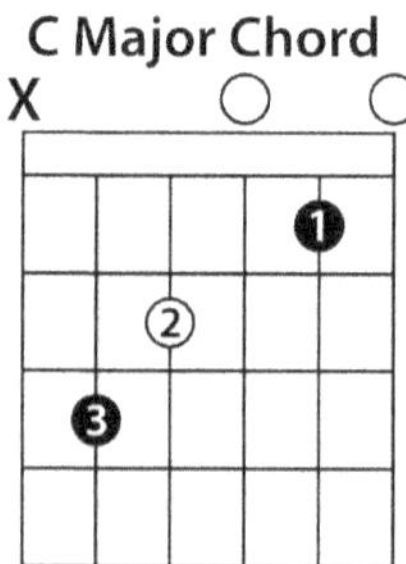

C Major Chord

The A Shape

Now, visualize the A chord and C chord together. The idea here is to superimpose the C major chord on the A chord shape. But you have to begin with the root note of the C chord, i.e., C key. Move a bit further up the fretboard to get a note that serves as the root note for the C major chord, but remains as close as possible to the lower part of the fretboard. See the illustration below.

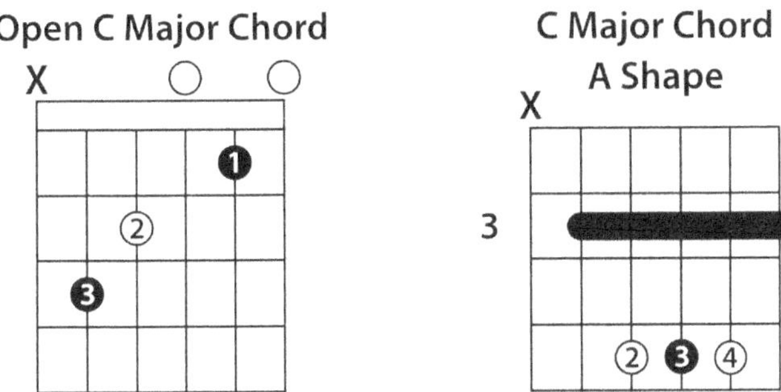

Open C Major Chord

Take note of the shape of the new chord.

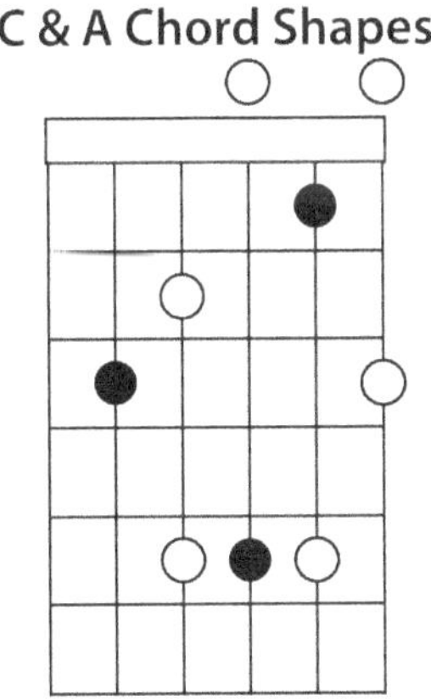

C and A Chord Shapes

The G Chord Shape

The G chord is next in the line. The same rule applies here. Using the new C major chord shape, play the G Chord on the A chord shape. However, take note of the root note: the root must be a note further up the fretboard from the A shape, but use that as the root note closest to the lower part of your fretboard in the G shape. Visualize both chords together on the fretboard to make it easier.

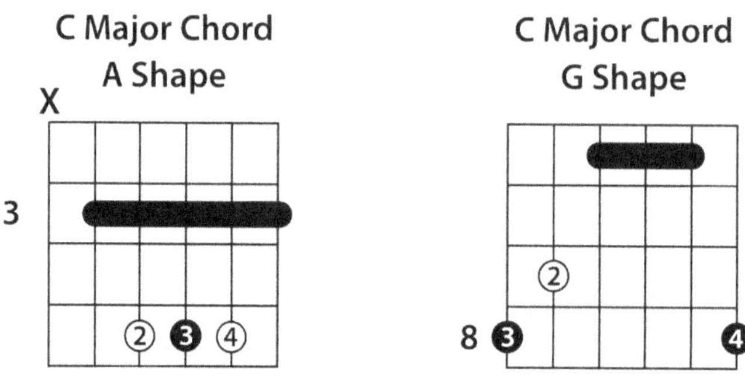

C Major Chord in A Shape   G major Shape

The E Shape

The next chord is the E major chord. It's the same as the normal open E major chord shape. As always, visualize both chords together and be sure of the root notes positions before merging.

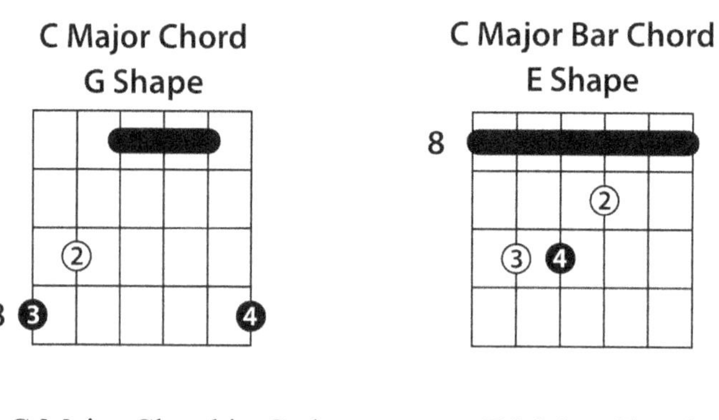

C Major Chord in G shape   E Major Chord

The D Shape

This is the last Chord in the CAGED system. So here, we continue from the last Chord shape and play the D major chord in the E shape. The highest root note in the E shape is used as the lowest root note in the D shape. As you move around the fretboard, be sure that the sound of the chords is coming out clearly.

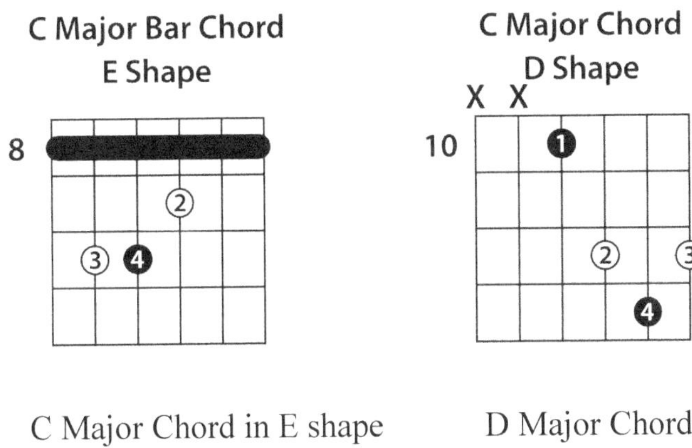

C Major Chord in E shape   D Major Chord

Points to note:

1. *Always be mindful of the root note as you move along the fretboard.*

2. *Before moving on to the next shape, be sure to note the shape of each one for easy memorization.*

Chapter 4

More on Chords

Chord Voicing

In line with what has been discussed in the last two chapters, I think it is important to also show you how to create alternate voicings to the chords you've learned so far. I suggest you take your time and learn and memorize enough fretboard notes and chord shapes, as this will make your journey from here on easier. Chord voicing introduces you to a technique used to express a given chord in more unique ways based on the order in which the tones of that chord are stacked. For instance, an A major chord can be played in the open position as well as an E shape barre chord.

Simply, chord voicing is just another way of playing or expressing a known chord based on its inherent notes to produce better sounds or versions of that chord. In chord progressions, knowledge of various forms of voicing a particular chord is essential. Note that each voicing is unique but based on the original chord position. In essence, you don't have to rely on only one chord shape. Building different chord voicings allows you to improvise and create more interesting harmonies, and change from one chord shape to another with greater ease and flexibility. Based on the chord types discussed in the last chapter, let's look at a few chord voicings.

Major 7th Chord Voicings

Taking, for example, the fingering of the major 7th chords, you'll see below some other voicings for expressing the same notes on this chord. Remember, the major 7th chord is the first group of extended chords: having 4 notes, including the root, 3rd, 5th, and 7th. The diagram shows the natural way of playing the chord, with the root note being in the high F string, but as we see in the second illustration, the root note can be taken from a different pitch higher up the fretboard. Note that the 5th and 7th-degree notes are higher up in the second voicing.

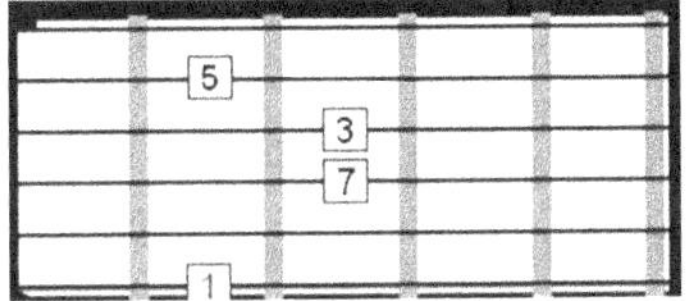 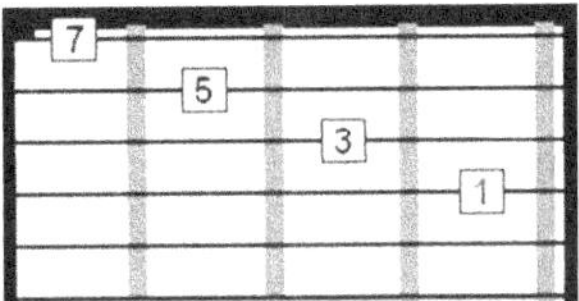

Minor Added 9ᵗʰ Chord Voicings

Once more, remember the added chord category. For the minor added 9th chords, the highest note is the 9th, but it does not include the 7th note. The typical chord structure for the minor 9th chords is 1, b3, 5, 9 (no 7th note). Below are two unique ways of voicing these types of chords.

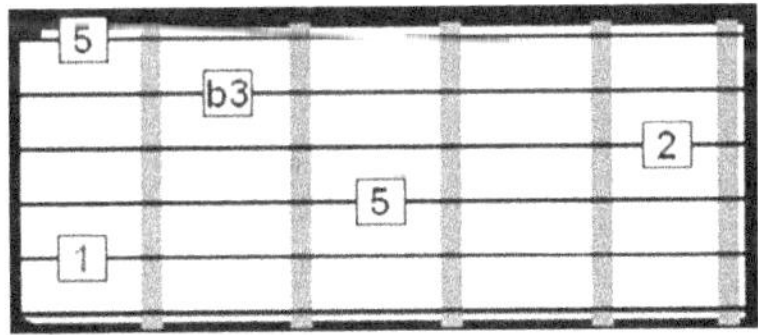

Below is a second voicing of the same chord.

The examples given above are simply the tip of the iceberg. For all the chords known to you, there are many voicings you can create for them so that unique sounds are generated from existing chords without necessarily altering the structure of the chords. And again, this technique allows you to be freer on the fretboard. The challenge of swiftly changing from one chord to another. Finding chord progressions is practically overcome because once you master this, it means you know the fret board almost totally.

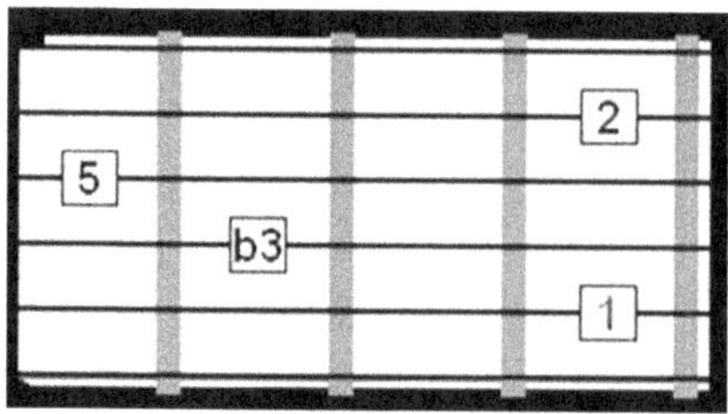

13ᵗʰ Chord Voicing

Looking back at when I discussed dominant 13th chords in chord extension, remember that dominant 23rd chords have a **root note, 3rd, 5th, m7th** (minor 7th), **9th,** and **13ᵗʰ** notes. The charts below show two other ways of playing (voicings) the dominant 13th chord. Since the chord stacks up more than four notes, you won't be able to get all 6 notes under your fingers. So, you can drop the 5th and root notes as they won't alter the harmonious sound of the chord. Besides, in practical situations, if you're playing with a group of the band, listen to know if the 5th note is being played by the bassists, as that will mean you do not need to bother including it at all. This chord can be played in a 1 5 6 4 progression.

The next diagram illustrates another way to play the same chord. Pay attention to the new positions of the notes on the fretboard. When played, you'll obtain a different sound compared to the first one.

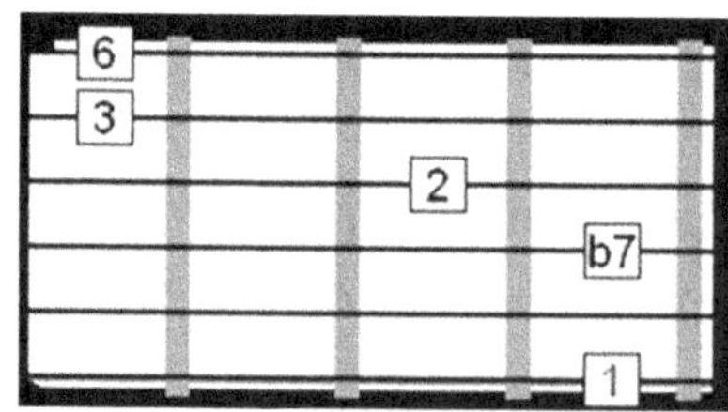

When written down, the chord construction for both shakes will be 1ˢᵗ 5ᵗʰ b7th 3ʳᵈ 6ᵗʰ 2ⁿᵈ and 1ˢᵗ b7ᵗʰ 2ⁿᵈ 3ʳᵈ 6ᵗʰ.

Note that these are just two ways of voicing this particular chord. There are other voicings. With practice, you can build and master more of them.

Some things to keep in mind are:

- Always know the root note of every chord you play. It is easier to find an alternative root note on the fretboard.

- Begin your voicing practice by first playing the open positions of the chords you want to voice.

- You can add, remove, sharpen, or flattened different notes to get richer sounds.

- Experiment with as many voicings as possible, and stick to the patterns that fig your song better.

Chord Inversion

Chord inversion simply entails the reshuffling of the component notes of a standard chord such that the root note of the chord becomes any of the other notes in the chord. For example, the triad C major Chord is structured as root, 3rd note, and 5th note, i.e., C, E, and G. When we invert this chord, we can obtain a new sequence such as G, C, E or E, G, C. These new chords are called inversions of the natural chord position. Just as discussed in the previous section, chord inversion like chord voicing is aimed at producing the same effect of better harmony, flexibility, and improvisation. You don't have to sound boring or monotonous. It becomes easier to create your own songs and change from one chord to another.

Chord inversion is typically used on triad chords (3 note chords), but it can also be applied to 7th chords i.e., chords with four notes. Using the example I gave above, the first chord (G C E) becomes the 1st inversion while the second (E G C) becomes the 2nd inversion. But in practice, a major triad with the 3rd in the root note position is the first inversion, while the second inversion has the 5th in the root note position. Thus, in essence, a chord inversion involves the replacement of the root note of a chord by a note within the chord scale, thereby giving that note the position of the lowest note in that chord. One interesting benefit of chord inversion is that it allows you to play a chord in several other positions on the fretboard without necessarily sticking to the traditional chord shape.

Major Triad Chord Inversions

Let's use a G major chord, for example. Remember that a major triad chord has three notes: root, 3rd, and 5th notes. Hence, for a G major triad chord, we have G(1), B(3), and D(5). The G is the root or lowest note in the chord. It is also referred to as the bass note.

There are two voicings of this note in the root position. First is 1 3 5, and secondly 1 5 3. These voicings are called root positions because the root note is the bass or lowest note on the chord. In the first, the 3rd note is naturally built on the root, while in the second, the 5th note is built on the root note. You'll notice that both new chord positions sound alike because they're both based on the root note, though the 1 3 5 position sounds lower. You'll find that this is merely different voicings, as we are particularly interested in the change of the root note position when it comes to inversions. Remember, we said earlier that inversion occurs only when one of the notes other than the root note assumes the position of the lowest note in the chord, i.e., the root note is stacked up at a higher position.

1st Inversion

To get a 1st inversion of the G major triad chord, we simply make the 3rd note the root note and stack up the 5th and root notes above it. Hence, it becomes

B(3) D(5) G(1)

So to play this chord, we simply find the root note of the G major chord on any of B, G, or D strings. First, let's try to finger the root position of the H major chord before playing the Inversions. Make a root position for the G chord by placing your 3rd finger behind the 5th fret of the 4th string (G string), then place your 2nd finger behind the 4th fret of the 3rd string (D string), and your 1st finger behind the 3rd fret of the 2nd string (A string). Note that the note being played with your 3rd finger is the lowest or first note of the chord, which is a G. This is the root position of the G chord on the G string.

Now, let's play the 1st inversion of this chord. Simply move your 3rd finger off the 4th string and place it behind the 3rd fret of the 1st string. Still keep your other two fingers in place. While maintaining the positions of the other two fingers as they were in the standard chord shape, play these three notes. Note the difference in sound compared to the G major chord in root position. This is the first inversion of the G major chord. If you observe closely, you'll see that the lowest note is the B, which you're playing with your 2nd finger on the 4th fret of the 3rd string. As illustrated above, B is the 3rd note, which has now become the bass note.

2nd Inversion

To play the second inversion, we have to move the 5th note to the lowest position, and the root and 3rd above it. In this case, the 5th becomes the bass note.

D(5) G(1) B(3)

When you play this new chord position, note the difference between it and the 1st inversion. Note that they're a bit similar, except for the changes in positions of the root note.

Minor Triad Chord Inversions

To keep things fully in perspective, let's also consider inversions for a typical minor triad chord. You'll also recall that a minor triad chord is composed of a root (1), minor 3rd (b3), and 5th (5). Note that the difference is a flattened 3rd-degree note. Still using our G chord (though now a G minor chord) the root chord positions or voicings will be:

1(G) b3(Bb) 5(D) and 1(G) 5(D) b3(Bb)

All we need to do here is simply flatten the 3rd note to make a minor chord. This is achieved by fretting the note just one fret below the position of the corresponding note in the G major chord shape. (So, you'll place your 2nd finger behind the 3rd fret of the 3rd string).

1st and 2nd Inversions

To get the 1st inversion for a minor triad, the minor 3rd becomes the bass, while the 5th and root notes are stacked above it.

b3(Bb) 5(D) 1(G)

To get the second inversion, we follow a similar arrangement, as discussed above, for major chords. The 5th note takes the bass or lowest position, while the root and minor 3rd are placed above it, respectively. As you play, take note of the different positions and sounds of each inversion.

For the C major chord, we have the standard chord shape, 1st, and 2nd inversion as C E G, E G C, and G C E. You may build a chart for as many other chords of interest and practice with those. Being able to play more and more chord inversions is what differentiates you from a beginner who knows only one way to play known chords. Besides, it solidifies your knowledge of the fretboard, as well as enhances your flexibility as a player.

Basic Chords

Up until now, we have only mentioned major chords in examples and mostly in chord construction. Perhaps it will serve the reader some more good to delve further into the nature and use of the most important chords every guitar player uses. Your guess will obviously be that these are the simplest chords. Yes, you're right, but not all are basic chords. However, to keep things simple, we'll focus more on the more common ones, especially those you'll find necessary often. These chords are called triads. We have previously looked at the structure of triads under chords construction. Triads are a combination of three notes: the root, 3rd, and a perfect 5th note. They are generally the first chords every beginner guitarist encounters. So, it is important that you learn triads in their entirety, if possible, because your knowledge of advanced chords will be built on what you know of them. Besides, chord voicing and inversion may be difficult until you understand triads better.

Triads can be either major or minor, depending on the nature of the 3rd note in the chord scale. Other forms of triads are:

- Diminished triads: consist of a root, minor 3rd, and a diminished fifth.

- Augmented triads: consist of a root, major 3rd, and an augmented fifth. (Refer to the discussion on intervals for further details).

Major Triad Chords

These are otherwise known as major chords. We have already established that triads are built of three notes or pitches, which are a root note, a 3rd-degree note, and a perfect 5th note. For major triads, the third note is usually a major 3rd. Major chords are sometimes described as happy chords because of the harmonic sounds they produce. They form a very important group of chords in music generally. A-C major chord, for example, comprises only three notes based on the formula (1, 3, 5) given above.

C	D	E	F	G	A	B	C
1	2	3	4	5	6	7	8

Octave

C major = 1 3 5
           C E G

The three notes highlighted below the scale shown above make up the C major chord. With a good understanding of the fretboard, you can play this note on any part of the fretboard. What's most important is locating the root note, and then stacking the other notes above it. We can also say that all major chords are built from the major scale. In writing major chords, the practice is usually to write the Chord in just capital letters as in C or C major. The following are examples of major chords and their respective positions on the fretboard.

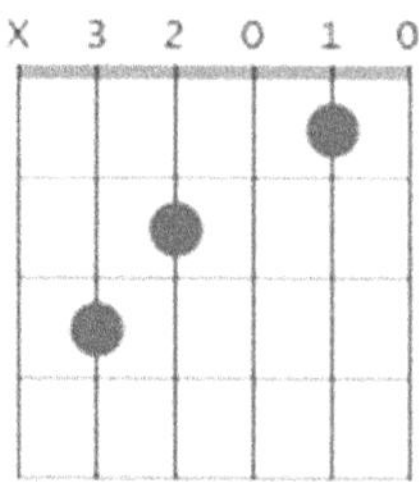

The C major Chord

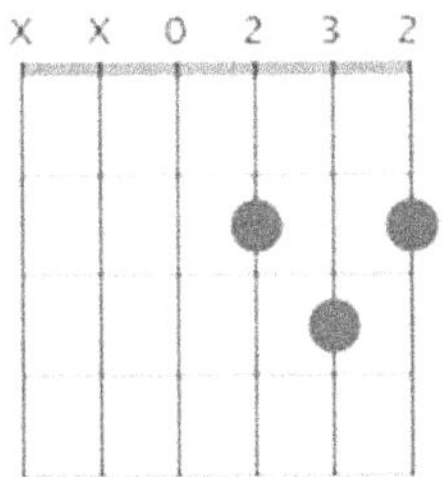

The D major Chord

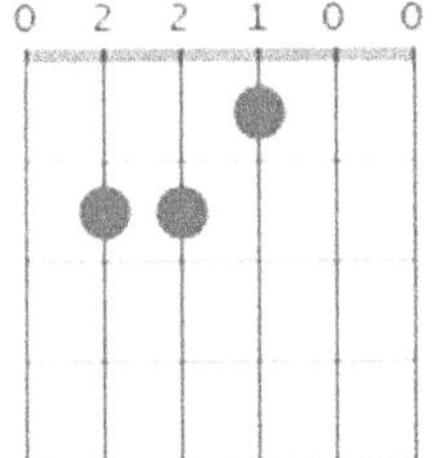

The E major Chord

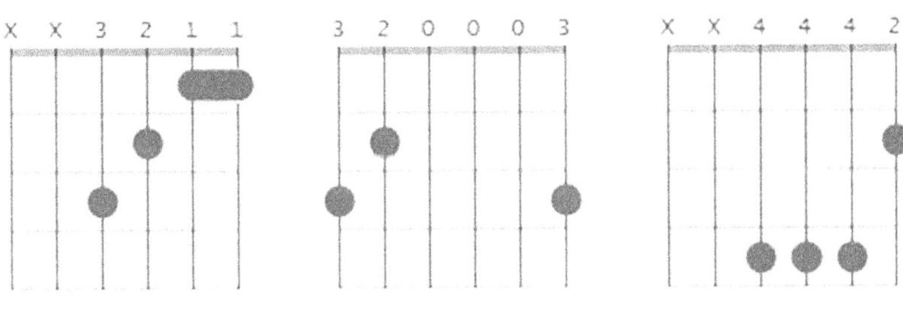

A major Chord   G major Chord   B major Chord

To play the C major chord, simply place your 1st finger behind the first fret of the 2nd string, then place your 2nd finger behind the second fret of the 4th string. Next, you place your 3rd finger behind the third fret of the 5th string. Play the notes together. Ensure that there's no buzz or dull or odd sound from any of the strings. Work your way like this through the rest. Then practice changing from one chord to another in a slow rhythm at first. As you begin to master the shape of each chord, you may then increase your tempo.

It's important to note that some of the component notes of the chords outlined above are sharp notes. For example, the 5th note of the A major chord is a C#. Also, for easy memorization, try to visualize the root notes of each chord. The major chords include the 7th major chords, which contain four notes, the 9th major chords (5 notes), 11th major chords (6 notes), and 13th major chords, which contain 7 notes. All these are added and extended chords built from the major chords.

The Minor Triad Chords

These are simple and easy derivatives of the major chords. What you do is simply flatten the 3rd major note by dropping its position one step or semitone on the fretboard. The general formula for minor triad chords is: 1 b3 5

So they have the root note, a flat or minor 3rd note, and a 5th note. In this case, fretting the C minor chord entails only one change: instead of fretting the 2nd fret of the 4th string, you place your 2nd finger on the 1st fret of that same string. That's how you flatten the third major note. The structure and shapes are basically similar except for the flattened major 3rd.

Essentially they too have a unique sound. Therefore, you need to listen to the difference in sound compared to the major notes. Minor triads are simply called minor chords and are written as Emin or Em (for an E minor chord).

So, in total, you have 14 basic or triad chords to play around with. Of these fourteen, you need to pay close attention to the C, A, G, E, and D chords - both minor and major. The reason is these are the chords you'll encounter more often, and learning them makes it much easier for you to improvise and voice other chords better. Besides, the minor chords of these chords are easier to play. Remember the lesson in the CAGED system. Guitarists use this technique to play a chord that is not restricted by the tones of open strings. They are built on these five fundamental chords.

Barre Chords

Barre chord is another name for a 'moveable chord.' Barre chords, also known as bar chords, are played by using one or more fingers (usually the index or middle finger) to hold down or bar several strings on a particular fret. They are essentially the kind of chords that you play anywhere across the fretboard. The finger or barre serves as a kind of nut or capo, forming the base of the chord shape, and allowing the player to move it (the barre) up the neck. Barre chording technique is a difficult one for beginners, but a guitarist who masters the technique of barre chords will find it easier to play chords that would otherwise be difficult to play by moving the chord to a different location on the fretboard. They can be moved up or down the fretboard. Mastering barre chords enables you to play any major or minor chord.

Important Barre Chord Shapes

There are basically two types of barre chords: some use only five strings. This type is derived from A major and on A minor chords. The second category uses 6 strings and is derived from E minor chords shapes. Barre chords can be played on several positions on the fretboard by sliding over several steps. Take the E minor chord shape; for example, it naturally has the shape of a barre chord. The nut of the guitar acts as the capo or bar while the fretting of the chord starts from the very first fret. See the illustration below.

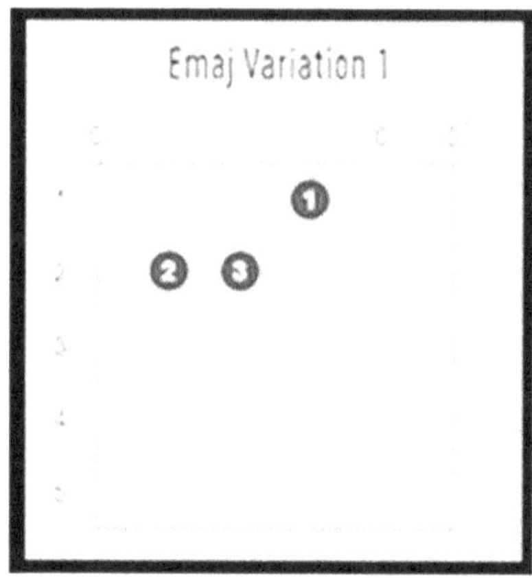

If we move the E major shape up by one fret and use the first or index finger to press down or bar all the strings behind the first fret, the resulting chord is an F major barre chord, as shown below.

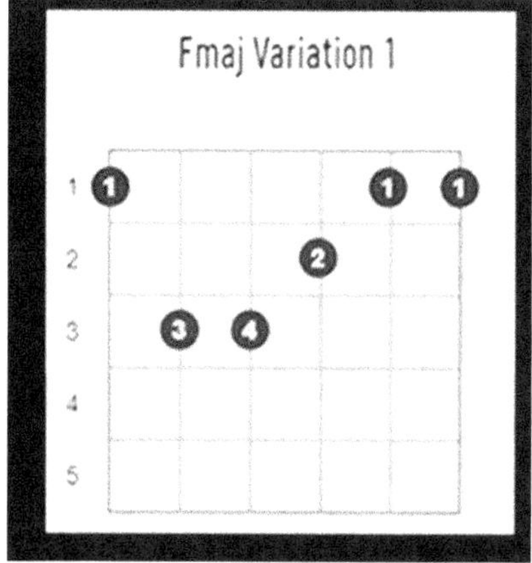

Again, if we move the chord shape further up the fretboard by one fret, i.e., you now press down all the strings behind the second fret, you'll get a G major chord instead. The amazing part is that you can practically create any chord shape you like on any position of the fretboard by using this technique

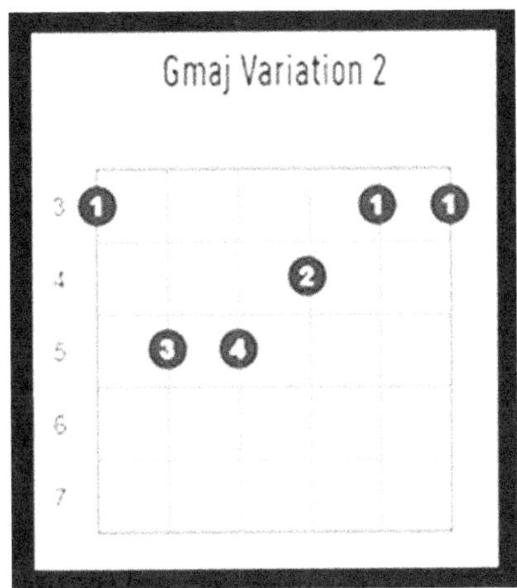

The E Barre Chord Shapes

It is important to note that the root note of the chords is on the 6th string. In fact, this is the easiest way to identify barre chords (by looking at their root or bass notes). The standard E major chord played in the open position is a barre chord. To achieve this, you place your first finger behind the G string, place your 2nd finger behind the 3rd fret of the D string, and then place your 3rd finger behind the 2nd fret of the A string. Play the notes. What you have is an E major chord (in an open position). See the diagram below for visualization.

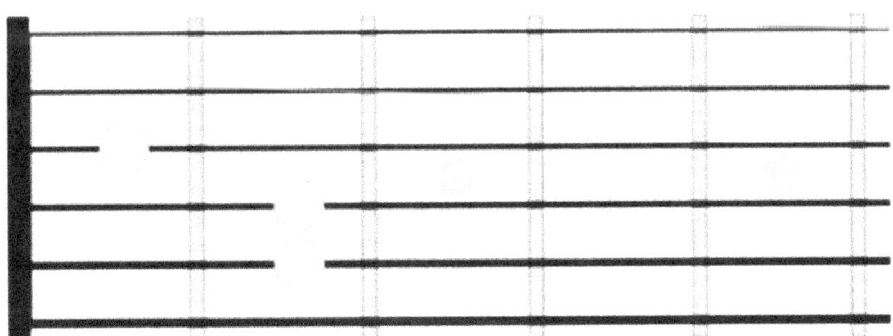

When we move this chord shape up the fretboard by one fret, i.e., we just shift one fret forward along the fretboard, and barre the index finger to represent the nut of the guitar, then what we have is a barre chord - an **F major barre chord**. When you move to the second fret, you get an **F# major barre chord**, and finally, a **G major barre chord** by the time you the same fingering to the 3rd fret. Based on the E minor chord shape, we can also play an **F minor barre chord** and so on. In this case, we simply lift the 2nd finger from the major shape to get the minor chord shape. Now, move the chord shape you have one fret up to get the **F minor barre chord**. You can proceed to play the higher chord by following the same process outlined above.

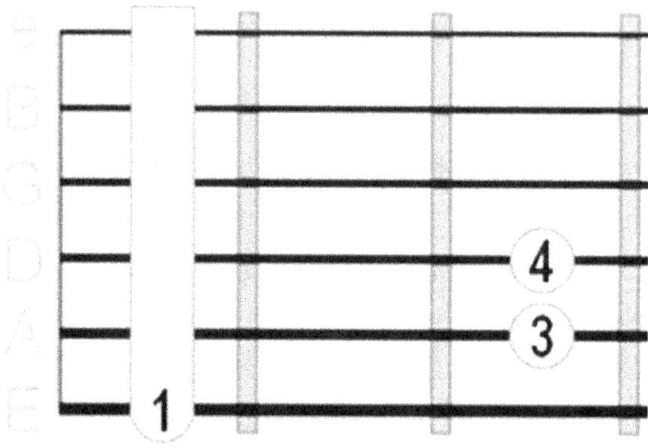

E minor Chord

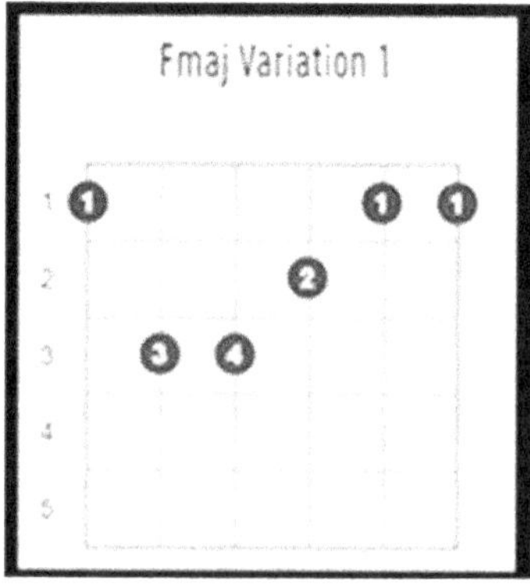

F minor barre chord

A Barre Chord Shapes

The A major chord shape is the important base chord for playing barre chords. The procedure is exactly the same as above, only you have to take note of the root (bass) note of the A major chord, which is on the 5th string this time. Remember, the chord is played in the open position. Once you move the fingering one fret up, you get a B major barre chord, as shown below. Here, you press down the 2nd, 3rd, and 4th strings with your third finger (ring finger) behind the 4th fret, and place the first finger behind the 2nd fret of the 5th string. You only need two fingers for fretting the B major barre chord. Although it may seem clumsy as you begin, it becomes easier as you play it repeatedly.

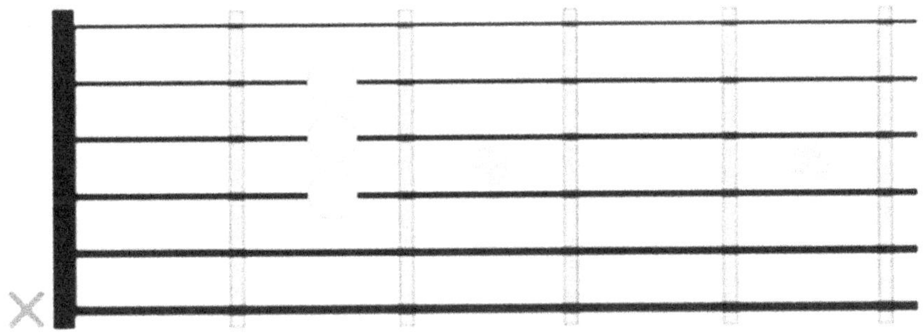

A major chord

To obtain the B minor barre chord shape, simply release the 3rd finger from the 3rd and 2nd strings, but leave it behind the 4th fret. Now, place your 2nd finger behind the 3rd fret of the 2nd string and your 4th finger behind the 4th fret of the 3rd string. Finally, let your first finger be the barre, i.e., it should rest on the 1st and 5th strings. The chord is played without sounding the 6th string. What you have played is a **B minor barre chord**. If you observe closely, you'll see that the shape of both the B minor barre chord is quite similar to that of F major barre chord. The difference is that the root note of the B minor chord is on the 5th string, and the entire chord is moved down one string, leaving out the 6th string.

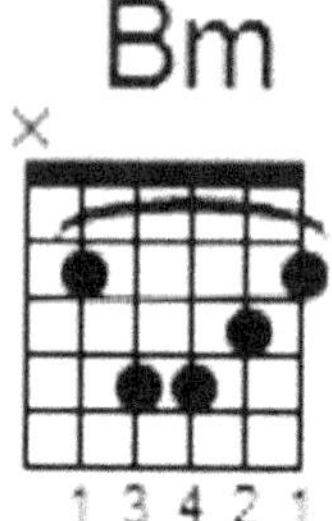

<table>
<tr><td style="text-align:center">B major barre chord</td><td style="text-align:center">B minor barre chord</td></tr>
</table>

Tips to note:

1. *Pay attention to the root note position*

2. *Start slowly before picking off the pace, but most importantly, try to memorize the shapes of the chords.*

3. *When playing the B major barre chord, you may use the 3rd finger as the barre, if you can't use the 1st finger.*

Playing barre chords is one of the essential techniques you'll need as a guitarist. We've only discussed the A major, A minor, E major, and E minor barre chord shapes, but there are others, though less commonly used. You may need to take some time to study these as they are very important.

Power Chords

If you love listening to rock music - soft, hard or metallic - and you love the sounds you hear, especially those low aggressive and muffled thump sounds, then you've heard power chords. So, it's time to dig into what makes a power cord, and how to play power chords. Power chords are essential, not just in rock music, but also in jazz, country music, and other genres. They have been used in many iconic riffs. It is one of the most powerful skills you'll need on your guitar.

Power chords are basically diads - comprising only two notes. Remember, we said earlier that triads are the most basic chord forms ever. Well, that is still true because power chords, though having just two chords, are not exactly chords in the real sense of the word. To begin with, they're neither major nor minor chords (the absence of the 3rd degree means you can't tell if it's a major or minor chord). They contain only the root note and 5th note of the main chords. Power chords are quite simple in their structure, but they present some level of difficulty in practice. However, as with other chord practice, you'll learn to get comfortable with them. As seen in the scale below, you'll notice that the chord name is written in a unique style - the letter of the root note alongside the number 5.

C	D	E	F	**G**	A	B	**C**
1	2	3	4	**5**	6	7	**8**

Root   Octave

So, by merely seeing the name of the chord, you can tell how to play it. Another important fact is that they are usually formed on the 5th and 6th strings because the notes on those strings ring out deeply. Also, they often involve some barring, meaning that you'll need an understanding of barre chords in these scenarios. Finally, they're movable, as expected for barre chords, and you can play them anywhere along the fretboard. In essence, to play any power chords, you'll need to know the root notes of the corresponding major scale and be versed in your understanding of the fretboard. For example, to find the notes in a C5 chord, you will have to know the root and 5th notes of the C major scale. Practically, that chord will have C and G keys.

Playing Power Chords

As mentioned earlier, power chords are mostly played on the low E and A strings (i.e., 5th and 6th strings) for best effects. Let's explore some common options.

Power Chords on the Low E (6th) String

For example, let's look at the fingering for a G power chord (G5). Place your 1st finger behind the 3rd fret of the 6th string (This a G note - the root note of the chord). Next, place your 3rd finger behind the 5th fret of the 5th string, then finally place your 4th finger beneath the 3rd, just behind the 5th fret of the 4th or D string (this note isn't exactly part of the chord, as it is only a higher octave of the root G note. This, however, makes the sound fuller altogether). One more trick to get the right sound out of this chord is to let your 1st finger rest softly on strings 3, 2, and 1. Those notes ought not to sound, so they should be muted. The sound will ruin the harmony of the chord if you let them ring out. Getting this shape under your fingers will be hard at first, but keep at it. See illustrations below for the guide.

G Power Chord

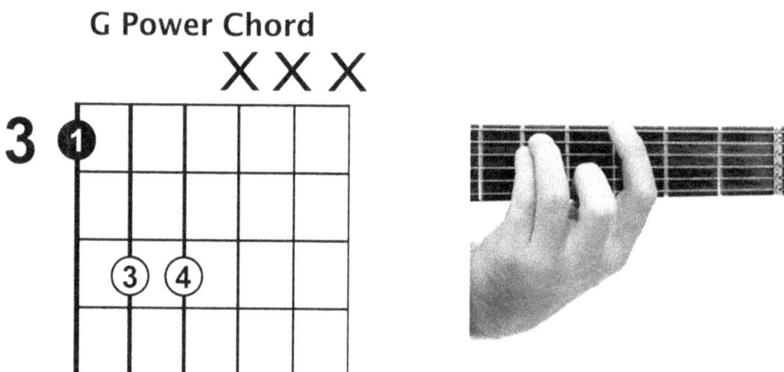

A downward strum should do the job. You can incorporate an upward strum if you feel the need. Now, this chord shape is moveable, meaning that you can play it anywhere on the fretboard, as long as you can locate the root note. Hence, you have another reason why you should master the notes on the fretboard. Since power chords are moveable, you can move the G chord up two frets to get the A power chord. You can get other chords as you move along the fretboard.

Power Chords on the A (5th) String

As mentioned earlier, the root note of a power chord can also be obtained on the A string. For example, consider the fretting of the C power chord. Begin by placing your 1st finger behind the 3rd fret of the A string (this is the root C note). Proceed by placing the 3rd finger behind the 5th fret of the D string. Again, place the 4th finger beneath the 3rd, just behind the 5th fret of the 4th string. This last note is a C note one octave higher than the root C note and serves to bring out a richer sound in the C power chord. Remember to mute the 3rd, 2nd, and 1st string by resting your 1st finger lightly on all of them. Note that the barring technique is the same for both the C5 and G5 chords.

C5

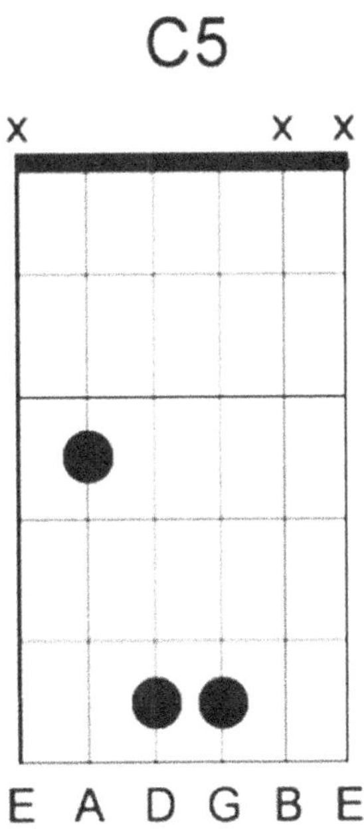

Power chords are usually needed for different occasions. If you actually look forward to creating great rock sounds, you can't, by any means, ignore power chords. They are some of your best techniques. Learning a few will do you some good along the line. You can also extend the root of power chords you want to play on the A string; hold down the low E string behind the fret, where you have the root note of the power cord, which is on the A string.

Tips to note:

1. Open notes are never used in power chords. So, be sure to avoid leaving any note open.

2. When playing power chords, the note you play with your index finger should always be the root note.

3. The root notes are usually on the 5th and 6th strings, so you need to keep your chords majorly on these two notes to get the best sound.

4. Power chords are moveable

5. Listen to songs that have power chords in them. That way, you sharpen your ears to recognize power chords and also practice them.

6. Power chords are neither major nor minor chords. So, they sound unique.

Borrowed Chords

Borrowed chords present another nice opportunity to create sweeter sounds from your guitar. I am certain that by now, you must have mastered a good number of techniques on your fretboard. While that is a necessity, and strongly encourage you to do so, you can take things a notch higher by learning the theory behind borrowed chords.

Chances are, you've seen or heard them in use before, perhaps even played some. Getting a theoretical knowledge of them will embellish your skills in this aspect. In short, borrowed chords are one area in your guitar music endeavor that you can't ignore if you seek to grow.

The word "borrowed" does not necessarily mean borrowed and returned, as in the normal sense of the word. But it basically implies taking a chord outside of the natural key of that chord and playing it alongside the chord as a parallel key, for example, changing from C major to C minor.

When we say parallel, it simply means "on the same root note." A borrowed chord is a chord that is taken from a key of the same bass or root note as the main chord. We know that C major and C minor have the same tonic root of C. Hence, either of them can serve as a borrowed chord to the other. So, borrowed chords are a temporary switch from one key or scale to another, in a bid to embellish the sound you are creating. This can be a very rewarding skill in songwriting; you get the chance to be more creative in your chord progressions. So, let us consider a few common borrowed chords sequences.

Major IV to Minor IV Chord

Imagine that we have the following chords in the key of C major

C Dm Em F G Am B

I ii iii IV V vi VI

Each of those chords contains notes from the C major scale, which includes the natural C key, i.e., they have a common root note of C. This means that you could combine any of the notes from these scales to generate a good sound. Let's look at the common chord progressions of 1 - 5 - 4 (I V IV).

In the key of C major, the progression will be Cmaj - Gmaj - Fmaj. But we can as well use an F minor for the 4 positions since it is a more common variant. Hence the progression becomes Cmaj - G maj - F min. i.e., I V vi. So, the ending of the progression can be alternated between the F major chord and the F minor chord. This will be a perfect parallel chord, as the root notes in each of these chords are just the same. So, in this scenario, we can say that the minor 4 chords (F min chord) are borrowed from the parallel C minor key. Keep in mind that parallel keys have the same root note.

The idea here is to basically incorporate a different chord whose scale is of a similar key to that of the parent chord's root note. In essence, a major chord can be alternated with a minor chord with the same root note. The 4 chord itself is a natural minor chord. So, if we want to create an accompaniment for the 1 5 4 sequences, we simply change from the C major scale to C natural minor over the minor 4 (iv) chord. Once you understand borrowed chords and can apply them in your practice, your ability to change scales will improve.

bVI Chord

Similar to the minor 4 chords borrowed key discussed above, there's also the instance of the major chord built on the 6th degree, which is A ♭ on the C minor natural scale. See the illustration below for the chords on the C minor natural scale.

Cm D° Eb Fm Gm Ab Bb

i ii° bIII iv v bVI bVII

On the C major key, the Ab minor chord translates to a flat 6th degree (♭ VI).

So, if the bVI chord is being borrowed from a parallel minor key, the change can be done from the C major scale to C minor scale over that Ab major chord. Another example of this is Cmaj - Am - A ♭

maj - G7 (I -vi - ♭VI - V). There are several other combinations. You'll need to be able to distinguish the uniqueness of borrowed chords in terms of sound to enable you to know when to change scales.

bIII Chord

According to the chord scale above, you'll see that another example of a borrowed chord can be taken from the 3 (III) chord on the scale. In this case, the parallel 3 chord on the C minor scale is E♭ major. It is a flat 3rd-degree chord. Another example of a borrowed chord in this category would be Cmaj - Am - E♭maj - Gmaj (I - vi - ♭III -V).

ii° Chord

The ii chord is another practical example. The little circle written next to the Roman numeral indicates that it's a diminished chord. In line with the illustration, we can also borrow the 2 (ii) chord of the parallel minor key. So, what we'll get as C minor would be D diminished, written as Dm7♭5, and also called a half-diminished 7th chord.

Cm D° Eb Fm Gm Ab Bb

i ii° bIII iv v bVI bVII

bVII Chord

Again, we can also borrow the 7 (VII) chord from the minor chord scale. Once more, stay mindful of the fact that a parallel key essentially has the same root note as the parent chord or the chord into which you're borrowing a minor chord. Here, the major scale has a diminished 7th degree (vii°).

Therefore, the flat 7th degree (♭ VII) replaces the major or diminished 7th degree (vii°), as seen in C major. Other example is Cmaj - Gmaj - Fm - B ♭ 7 (I - V - iv - bVII) progression.

In summary, while I have only narrowed the explanation and examples here to the C major and C minor keys, there are five borrowed chord changes that you'll find more common in major key music (ii°, ♭ III, iv, ♭ VI, ♭ VII). Remember that these chord borrowings are on the Eon parallel minor keys. As you work on getting these chord changes under your fingers, you need to also learn the parallel keys to each root note.

Circle of Fifths

The circle of fifths, also called the circle of fourths, is a handy tool that every musician, including guitarists, ought to be familiar with. It is an important concept in music theory, though it can sometimes seem like a mystery when not understood. It has been in circulation for many years in contemporary jazz, violin music, and so on. In contemporary music, it is more often referred to as the circle of fourth. The tool provides you a quick glance at the key signatures (number and types of keys) in a song. It also allows for easy learning of chords and scales, especially for guitarists. Every musician is more likely to appreciate this concept once they learn its Importance.

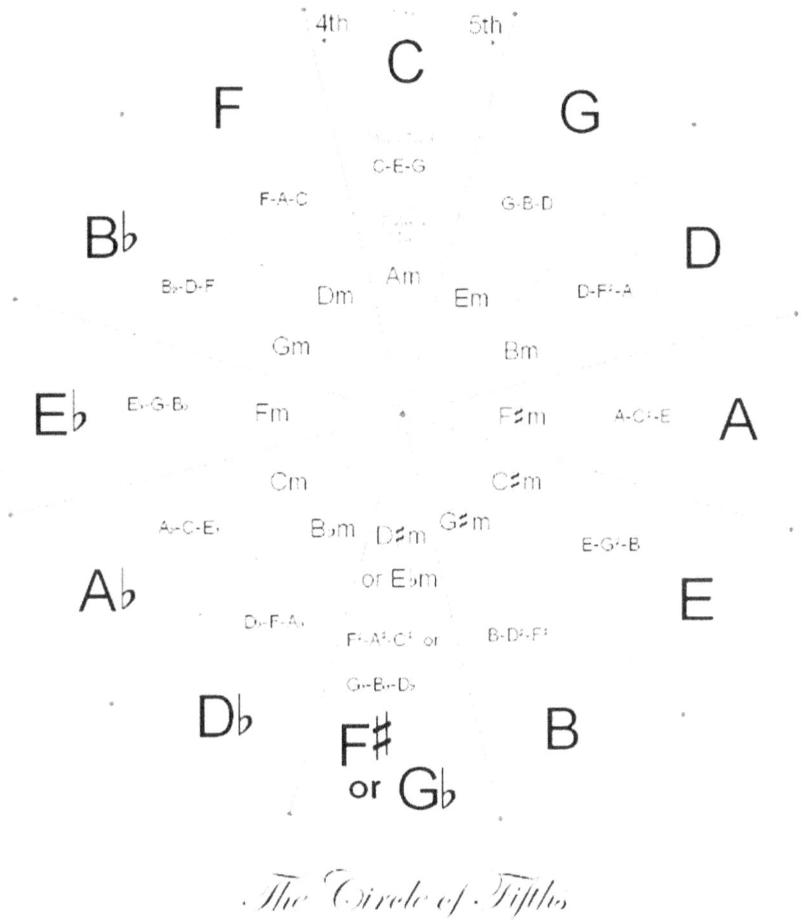

By definition, the Circle of Fifths is a musical tool that visually illustrates the relationships between all the 12 tones of the chromatic scale (the foundation of Western music). These notes are shown in a clockwise manner, at intervals of 5 notes, i.e., each note is a fifth (a perfect fifth above the previous note). And this is how the name is derived. The circle of fifths is primarily based on a music principle in which the circle begins from the note of C and the C Major key. This is because it has no sharps or flats. The notes repeatedly move up in steps, through every key, until it returns to C major again. The circle shows how all the musical notes and chords relate to each

other. The C major scale, for example, contains the following: C C#
D D# E F F# G G# A A# B. The fifth note of this scale is the G.
Now, the scale of the G major begins with key G and looks like this:
G G# A A# B C C# D D# E F F#. The next perfect 5th is A, so we
outline the scale and so on. All the other keys follow the same
progression. Notice that as you continue, with each fifth successive
scale, more sharps are seen.

The Order of Sharps and Flats

The order of sharps and flats that we see down the sequence makes it
easy to identify which five notes will be sharp or flat. Now, since the
sharps are cumulative, you'll see that the sharps appear in a fixed
order, as seen in the circle of fifths: F♯, C♯, G♯, D♯, A♯, E♯, B♯. The
number of sharps starts from zero at C and progresses to one at F,
and so on down the line.

On the order hand, when the circle is flipped the other way, we have
an order of fourths, i.e., the keys or notes repeat in order of fours,
and that's the order in which the flat notes appear: B♭, E♭, A♭, D
♭, G♭, C♭, F♭. Refer to the circle and see the key progression
clockwise and anticlockwise. Note that you'll need to create the
chromatic scales for each key to show the order of flats. Below is a
concise description of the sharps and flats you'll find in each key:

C has no #'s

G: 1 # = F#

D: 2 # = F#, C#

A: 3 # = F#, C#, G#

E: 4 # = F#, C#, G#, D#

B: 5 # = F#, C#, G#, D#, A#

F#: 6 # = F#, C#, G#, D#, A#, E#

C#: 7 # = F#, C#, G#, D#, A#, E#, B#

F: 1 b = Bb

Bb: 2 b = Bb, Eb

Eb: 3 b = Bb, Eb, Ab

Ab: 4 b = Bb, Eb, Ab, Db

Db: 5 b = Bb, Eb, Ab, Db, Gb

Gb: 6 b = Bb, Eb, Ab, Db, Gb, Cb

Cb: 7 b = Bb, Eb, Ab, Db, Gb, Cb, Fb

Benefits of the Circle of Fifths

In music, knowing the circle of Fifths or circle of fourths makes it easy to find key signatures for a scale or chord. When writing a song, your understanding of the circle of Fifths can help you understand modulations. For instance, to find the key signature of a song that is in F major, you want to know which sharps or flats to use. Let's look at our Circle of Fifths diagram.

To figure out the number of sharps or flats in F major, move around the Circle of Fifths clockwise. If we start at C and go around clockwise once, we land on G. This scale has one sharp, which is F♯. If we go around again, we land on D, so now we have two sharps: F♯ and C♯. But we need to find the flats in F major. So try moving the other way - counter-clockwise. Moving a perfect 5th from C, we arrive at F. Since we've only made one counter-clockwise move to end land F, then F has one flat. Note that it is flat this time, not sharp.

This is the pattern of notes around the Circle of Fifths. It is also the order in which sharps and flats are added to each key around the circle. Note that sharps go clockwise whereas, flats go counter-clockwise. These patterns in the Circle of Fifths are what makes it easy to find the key signature of any key. We can also see that the diagram, at a glance, showed how many sharps or flats are in each key, and their respective sequences, starting from the first note to the last key. It also tells you why you might choose one enharmonic equivalent over another.

Recall that enharmonic notes or keys are keys similar in sound are different in name. Here we see a big difference between a particular pair of enharmonic intervals. For example, For example, C# and Db are enharmonic keys - exactly the same note, but two different names. To make things clearer, you might choose a C#, for example, because it has 7 sharps, whereas Db has just 5 flats. Refer to the table above. In situations where you don't understand music scores, it is easier to blend in when you can identify or point out the number of flats or sharps in the score. For example, when you see 5 sharps at the beginning of the note staff, you'll know that the song is in the key of "B."

In summary, the Circle of Fifth can be used for

- Finding the key signature if any key, hence, it should be memorized if possible.

- Building scales

- Reading scales straight from the circle

- Building chords

- Playing chords progression

- Seamless manipulation of keys and chords in songwriting

Chapter 5

Essential Guitar Techniques

After mastering the fretboard, learning to fret notes with your left fingers, using a pick and learning chord techniques, there are other great and essential techniques every guitar player needs to get under their belt. This chapter is dedicated to discussing these techniques. Remember, the best way to master the guitar is by practicing every new technique you learn while taking cues from real-life examples as much as you can, and most importantly, learn one perfectly well before moving to another, especially the harder ones.

Strumming

Simply put, strumming is how you sound the chords you've learned in the preceding chapters. It is a technique that must be learned as it is essential to the quality of sound you produce. Great chord techniques and perfects strums are like two ends of a pole - they go hand in hand. While chord fingering is dependent on the strength and dexterity of the left finger, strumming or playing the chord is dependent upon how skillful you are with your right hand.

With an average to pro strength on both fingers, one can create a unique sound and style. Therefore, the need for a well-trained right hand can hardly be overemphasized. However, for the purpose of building the strength and skill of your right hand, you might want to stick solely to practicing the strumming techniques first. Get them understood first before fretting the chords alongside it.

Guitar strums are either played as downward strokes (from the last to the first string) or an upward stroke (from the first to the last or thickest string) to produce sound from your guitar. There are 5 basic strumming patterns that are based on a different combination of strokes, but just before we take them one at a time, take note of the following tips.

Important Tips you Need to Keep in Mind

- To get this quicker, you'll need to keep a pick handy. However, let your grip on the pick be natural. Whether you angle it upward, downward, or parallel to the strings, it doesn't really matter. All that's important is being comfortable and natural with your grip. You may refer to the fifth lesson in chapter one for further help on this. Regardless of how you want to hold the pick, it's important that you're comfortable!

- Let your movements swing from the wrist and not from the elbow. Your wrist must be flexible. You can pretend you really need to wiggle something off of your wrist. A bad strumming technique involves the swinging of the elbow. Avoid that to prevent striking out poor sounds or wearing out your hand.

- Finally, your hand should be free of tension. Be relaxed as much as you can be. If you begin to feel any tension in your fingers as you strum, take a break, relax your hands and fingers, and then start over again.

Basic Guitar Strumming Patterns

Each of these five patterns builds off the previous pattern. The strumming patterns you already know may be similar to these, but it's important to stick to the progression, especially if you are a beginner. In terms of real-life music, the strumming patterns covered here are eighth-note patterns with 4 beats. Most songs you hear are in 4/4 time, which is four even beats; quarter notes. When counting the notes, also call out the 'and' in-between, as in "one and two and three and…", and be sure to space them out evenly.

1 & 2 & 3 & 4 &

Also, take note of the strum notations illustrated below. There are three forms of notations: downstroke, upstroke, and muted stroke.

$\sqcap$ = Downstroke

$\vee$ = Upstroke

$\times$ = Mute

Downstrokes (Upstrums)

This is the first pattern and simplest pattern. The other patterns generally build from this. With your pick, make simple downward swings on the strings. Be sure to let the sound come out clearly. Strum over the hole in the box and close to the bridge. Allow your wrist to swing freely without tension. It's quite easy to begin playing this strumming pattern lightly, but you need to be firm as your sounds may end up low without energy.

Downstrokes and Up Strokes

The second strumming pattern is a combination of both downstrokes and upstrokes. It has the same rhythm as the first pattern, but this time, instead of using all downstrokes, we incorporate an upstroke. We swing down and back up to make a quarter note. So, we are alternating downstrokes and upstrokes, beginning with downstrokes. The points where you count the 'and' is where the upstrokes come in. Remember, the numbers are downstrokes while the ands are upstrokes.

It`s important to note that this strumming pattern is also foundational, as other patterns will build on it.

Remember, once again to keep your fingers relaxed and your wrist flexible. To help with the beat and tempo, you can use a metronome as you strum. Keep the strumming even and smooth. It's not necessary to capture all the strings with an upstroke. The top three or four strings will be fine.

Muted (Palm Mute) Strum

This pattern is similar to the second, only that it introduces a muted strum. As you do a downstroke for the muted strum, you let off the pressure with your fretting hand a little. The muted strum involves muting the strings with the palm of your strumming hand before strumming through the strings. The rhythm is similar to the two and four beats that a snare drum gives – that's what you should get if you do it right. The muted strum gives a drum-like sound to the strumming. A muted downstroke strumming pattern is used on beat two and then repeated on the third and fourth beats.

According to the illustration above, the second and fourth strums (the ones marked 'X') are muted periodically as you progress. As always, you can take things slow and pick up the pace as you master the technique. You`ll notice that the sound you get here is unique and has created a beautiful vibe.

At this point, you may begin to introduce the chord fretting so as to get a richer feel of the sounds. Chord changes can also be incorporated; start with the C to G chord and back again. As you master the strumming patterns, you can alternate between other common or advanced chords.

Strumming Without the Eight Notes

So far, the strumming patterns we have discussed have all the notes in our eight-note scale. Now, that`s a bit boring as most songs include advanced strumming, which involves leaving out the downstrokes at some point. In essence, learning some complicated chord strumming pattern is a technique you need to spice up your music.

In this case, the 'and' in-between the notes are left out. Normally, in the constant strumming pattern which we've discussed so far, the 'and' will be played as an upstroke, but this time, you just come back up without strumming the 'and' while keeping the upward motion intact.

Notice the sound produced. You can play this pattern repeatedly and with chord changes as well. Also, you may need to count as you play, just so you stay on track with the tempo and beat. Remember to keep your fingers and wrist relaxed, and the upstrokes do not need to involve all the strings.

Strums with Rests in the Third Note

This pattern is very much similar to the previous pattern. The difference lies in the omission of the third beat and reintroduction of the eighth note. The rest of the strumming is just as regular as before. Also note that it is the downstroke that is left out this time (remember the beat on the third strum is a downstroke); meanwhile, the downward motion is still intact even though we are not hitting the string.

⊓ V ⊓ V   V ⊓ V
1 & 2 & 3 & 4 &

Note that all of the strumming patterns discussed above are elementary. Once you get them down perfectly, you may begin to create your own strums or learn other advanced strumming patterns. As soon as you are confident enough, you can graduate to playing actual songs.

Tips to Note:

1. Be sure to hold your pick firmly but comfortably between your finger and thumb, so it doesn't slip, break or fall out of your hand.

2. Keep your elbows beside you and let the motion only come from your wrist.

3. Keep a loose wrist and relaxed fingers. Swing your wrist as though you are flicking something off from your fingers.

4. Begin first with the right fingers only, then gradually add the chord fingers as you strum

5. Count out the notes as you play, and as loudly as possible to keep track of the beat

6. You don't have to strike all the strings during an upstroke

7. Ensure that all the strings are ringing out clearly

8. Do not strum too hard or too softly either.

9. Build your strumming accuracy before developing your speed

10. Start with a low tempo when you begin switching chords. As you master chord fretting and strumming together, you may then gradually raise the tempo of your strumming.

String Muting and Damping

These are two techniques you'll need as either as a beginner or as a pro guitarist. These are part of the little touches that you introduce here and there to improve your overall sound. String muting and damping are particularly useful in rock and blues music. Simply, they are methods used to prevent strings that aren't needed from sounding (muting) or reduce the intensity of playing strings (damping). String muting is simply preventing some strings from sounding while other strings are played while string damping is stopping the playing strings from sound with their natural frequency so that a muffled sound is produced instead.

Muting ensures that unneeded strings do not interfere with the desired sound. Damping is a technique generally used in music for altering the sound of a musical instrument by reducing the instrument's vibrations or oscillations. In the case of the guitar, this is done by touching or simply pressing the vibrating strings with the right palm or by relaxing the left hand's pressure on the strings. The damping of strings is used to produce a unique kind of expressive sound from the strings. A polished sound is somewhat dependent on your ability to apply the string muting and damping techniques while playing. Unlike muting, damping retains the actual pitch of the notes in each string.

As you can figure, the ability to mute and damp string is essential.

How to Mute and Damp

The technique employed in both is similar – involves the use of the fleshy side of the right hand or the thump. The difference, however, is in the position of the hand. Though the position of the hand is different in both techniques, it is similar in relation to the strings. Another important thing to note is that muting and damping ought to be done close to the bridge of the guitar.

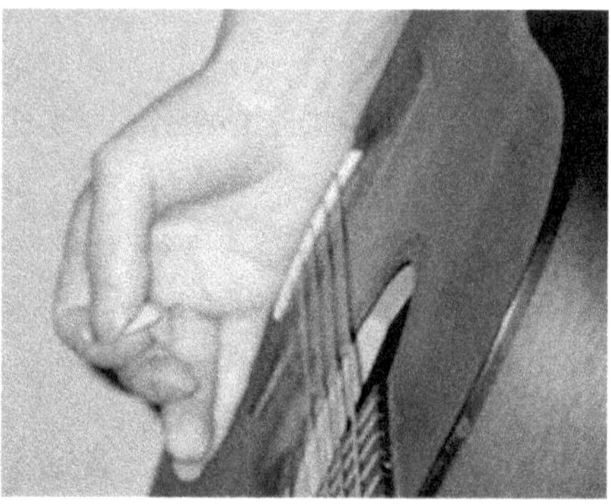

For muting, it does not matter where the hand is as long as the unwanted strings are muted. With the pick in your right hand, place your hand on the strings but leave some notes, say the first and second strings, to ring free. Now, brush across the strings with the pick.

For damping, simply place the side of your hand down on the strings by the bridge, and with the pick, sweep across the entire strings starting from the first to the last. Notice that the sound produced is muffled. Notice that some strings still sound clearly in when muting is done, unlike when the strings are damped. Also note that the damping can be partial, depending on which strings or note you want to ring out. The left-hand fingers, i.e., the fretting fingers, particularly the little finger, are also used in damping unwanted notes. To do this, you simply place your fretting fingers onto the specific string(s) you want to dampen after plucking them exactly when you want to stop the strings from vibrating. These techniques are common and widely used, so you need to give a little time to practice them as they will help your performance.

Hammer-Ons and Pull-Offs

Hammer-ons and Pull-offs are another set of great techniques used in playing the guitar. Hammer-ons and pull-offs add speed and fluidity to your playing, so you need them as well. Using the open G String, for example, place your index finger firmly behind the 1st fret, pluck the string, then quickly bring your 2nd finger down behind the 3rd fret of the same string, but this time, do not pluck the string. Once you execute this, you've played a hammer-on. If well done, you'll hear a very smooth progression of the notes.

Pull-off is just the exact opposite - more like a reverse movement. After fretting the 1st note, pluck it and fret the second note without releasing the first. While keeping the 2nd note fretted, release your 1st finger but do not fret the 2nd note. As you play this technique, listen to the progression of the notes. It should be smooth. Hammer-ons and pull-offs produce a legato sound, such that the notes connect smoothly. Both techniques are notated with a slur. Hammer-ons will slur to a higher pitch while pull-offs will slur to a lower pitch. It's like a forward and reverses progression. Both involve less picking, so you get to concentrate more on the fretting fingers.

String Bending

The bending technique also brings another sweet touch to your playing. Because it involves playing between pitches, it's a great technique that adds to your tone and lyricism. Begin by fretting the first note with your ring or 3rd finger. Choose any fret on the high E string, for example. Pluck the string and slide your finger vertically up or down (parallel to the fret) without raising your finger off the fretboard. This is called string bending. Sustain the bend until you hit a target pitch, i.e., the second note.

If you are sliding upward, you can support the ring finger by placing the middle and index fingers closely beside it. Then slide up to the case strings tagged, picking the first note. Typically, the higher you bend, the higher the pitch. These bends are measured in tones - semitones and wholesome. Note that it is important to practice correct bending as bending out of pitch sounds bad. You may extend your bending across several tones as necessary.

There's also a different twist to bending, called pre-bending. In this case, the bending of the note is done before plucking the strings. Then pluck the string and return to the first note. This can be done either by pulling down or pushing upwards.

Release, another technique in bending, is used to end a bent or pre-bent note. You start from an already bent or pre-bent note, pluck the note and return vertically up or down to an unbent note. This method is the reverse of bending it pre-bending.

Sliding

Slides are a great way to move from one note or pitch to another as smoothly as possible. Like hammer-ons and pull-offs, slides are regarded as legato sounds because they smoothly connect two notes.

To perform a slide, simply fret and play a note, then slide downwards or upwards along the fretboard on the same string without lifting a finger. Notice that the note produced has an interesting sound. Sliding downwards is toward the neck of the guitar, and that is a lower pitch. Sliding upwards is toward the bridge, and is raising the pitch if the note. Since you can only slide one string at a time, it's best to start with the index finger on the first string. Another type of slide called 'shift' slides involves plucking the string again on the second note or in-between a slide. These techniques are pretty easy to play. Most beginners often experiment on this without knowing. Keep practicing it until you get distinct and clear sounding notes.

Vibrato

Just as every singer has his or her natural vibrato, every guitarist needs to develop their vibrato. The reason is that the vibrato technique is one that gives a refreshing vibe to notes you play. It is usually performed on a single string to bring out the richness and depth of a specific note. Vibrato is a very personal yet expensive technique for guitar players. It is also foolproof.

To perform a standard vibrato, just fret or pick any note, let it ring, then gently push and pull the string up and down, using either the index or middle fingers. You may sustain the ring for as long as you feel necessary but keeping the finger firmly rested on the string.

This is an advanced technique, but it's easier to learn if you are able to get your string bending technique right. Placing the fretting hand thumb over the neck can also serve as a pivot here. Try practicing the vibrato at different speeds, width, and intensity to improve your dexterity and improvisation.

There are two types of vibrato techniques:

1. Method 1 – Pivot Vibrato. This type of vibrato is the most common and easiest to play. You pull the string downward while pivoting around the ball of your hand. Begin by fretting the note, then pluck the string you want to play. For balance and rhythm, you'll need to pivot your hand back and forth around the ball of your hand (where your fingers connect to your hand). It is better and easier to start first with the index finger and in the high E string. Then progress upwards as you gain mastery.

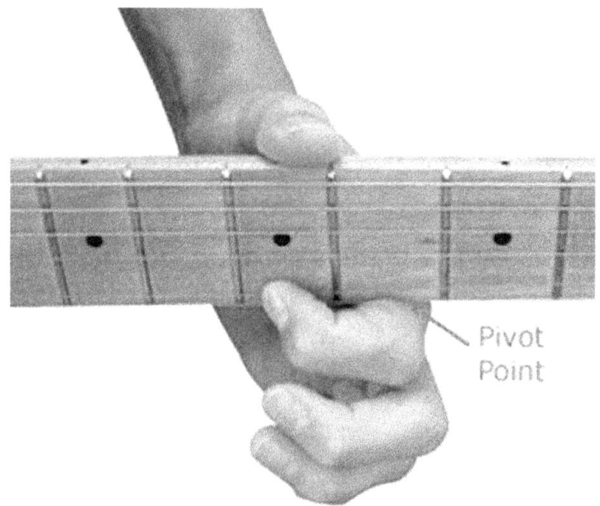

1. **Method 2 – Upward Vibrato**

This is similar to the first but finds application mainly when the pivot vibrato cannot be used to play an upward bent note. There are two types of upward vibrato: The first uses the weight of the guitar and the arm movement from the elbow up, while the second uses the hand muscles to produce the vibrato. In some cases, the weight of the guitar can help in producing the vibrato.

Another way to learn vibrato is to look at your favorite player. Watch their vibrato techniques and build yours. As always, it is essential not to rush things. Generally, different techniques give you different sounds and feel. You may use a combination of different techniques, as many as you can per time. However, be sure to master one before moving to another.

Alternate Picking

This technique helps guitarists get more economical in picking notes. It`s simple. Instead of picking notes with only downstrokes, you add upstrokes to your string picking. You can quickly experiment with your pick. With your pick, strike the strings from the first to the last with an up-down-up-down or down-up-down-up movement. Note that you`ll need balance and extra control to get the notes clearly and loudly without picking unwanted strings.

For beginners learning this technique, you`ll need to play to a jam track, metronome or beat, to help you stay on track and increase your tempo quickly. As soon as you get the technique under your fingers, it is time to extend your picking across the fretboard. Practice picking notes from different frets on the same string – close frets and widely separated frets. Then proceed to use alternate picking on different strings – for vertical and diagonal notes on the fretboard, i.e., by changing strings. You`ll find this twist particularly helpful when running scales and chord arpeggios. The idea behind alternate picking is just about improvising and improving the effectiveness of your right-hand fingers. For practice, refer to the below illustration for a guide.

8 10   7 8 7   7 8 10   7   10 8 10   7   9 10 9 7
               10   10   10

9 10   7 9 7   7 9 10   8   8   10   8   10 8
               10   10 9 10   8 10   10

10   7 8 10 8 7 8

The exercise is on the E major scale; the root note is on the 8th fret on the E string. Begin by alternately picking the 8th and 10th notes on the E string. Quickly switch to the A string. Note that there are three notes here. So, play the 7th fret, the 8th fret, and then the 7th again before moving on to 7th, 8th, and 10th notes. Move one string up to the D string, fret and pick the 7th note and return to the A string. Keep this up until the end of the scale. The pattern you just played is an ascending pattern for alternate picking. You`ll need patience and focus to master this. Below is another exercise, but this time, you`ll play in descending order, and you begin at the lower E string. Follow the progression of the scale run until the end.

8 7   7
     10 8 10   10 8   8
                         10 9 10   10 9 7   7 9 7
                                               10   10

9 7 9 10 9 7   7
               10 8 10   10 8 7   7 8 7
                                   10   10 8 7 8

While you are at it, ensure that your switch between strings is smooth and seamless. Until you achieve this level of fluidity, you may need to continue practicing the technique.

Sharps and Flats

We have used the terms sharps (♯) and flats (♭) several times in discussions before now. That's because they're essential in guitar music and music in general. A robust understanding of what they are and how to apply them in music will go a long way toward sealing your mastery of the fretboard. Here, let's take a closer look at their origin, what they are, and how they appear across the fretboard.

Altering Natural Notes in Scales

Sharp and flat are terms refer to a note or chord that is raised or lowered by an interval of a half step or semi-tone. Sharps and flats come into a scale when we flatten or sharpen a note, thereby altering the natural sound of that note. The roles of sharps and flats in music theory is best visualized when you study how they appear in relation to scales. For example, see the below.

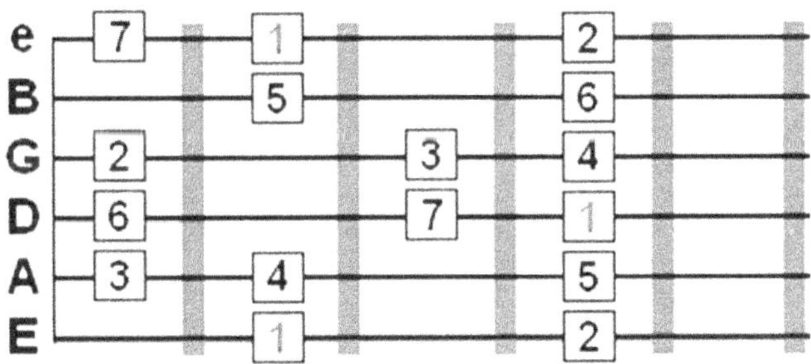

A major scale has 7 natural notes: **1 2 3 4 5 6 7**. The notes are also known as intervals when we think of their distances apart on the fretboard. In other words, each note represents an interval. The major scale is fundamental to music theory and can be described as a scale with no sharp or flat intervals. The major scale is a starting point for creating other scales in guitar music. Sharps and flats will, therefore, arise in any scale when you raise or lower natural intervals in the major scale positions, thereby creating new scales. Examples of such new scales is the minor scale.

Note: *The altering of the original positions of these intervals creates sharps (#) and flats (b).*

Here's another example: if you moved the 7th tone of the major scale down by one fret or semitone, the new 7th note is known as a flat 7th or minor 7th **(b7)**. You've just flattened or lowered the 7th by one semitone or half step, thereby creating a new flat 7th note; and by extension, a flat 7th scale. The new scale will become: **1 2 3 4 5 6 b7**

In music theory, the flat 7th scale – the new scale - has a name of its own - the **Mixolydian scale**. The only difference between the major scale and Mixolydian scale is just in one tone – the 7th note.

Now, if we go back to the original major scale pattern and sharpen a natural tone, say the 5th note. We do this by raising the tone a semitone or half-step higher than the original tone (remember that on the fretboard, a half-step is simply one fret up or down). This is the opposite of flattening the tone, so this time we move it up one semitone to create a **sharpened 4th (#4)** note. We will get a new scale, which is known as the **Lydian scale**. The Intervals in the new scale will have the following interval: **1 2 3 #4 5 6 7**

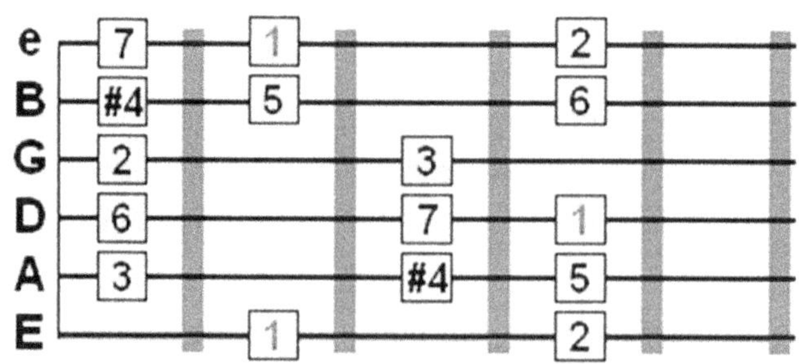

So, it's easy to see that sharps and flats take their roots from the original positions of natural tones in the major scale. The same applies to all major scales irrespective of the key of that scale. We also see that minor scales are a derivation of major scales.

Note: You can create as many scales as you want by using combinations of sharps and flats, which is what gives a scale its unique and interesting sound.

Altering Natural Notes in Chords

Since chords are formed from scales, the same applies as we see in scales; sharps and flats also exist within chord forms. Recall that chords are a selection of tones or notes out of a scale - some are made of three tones, some four, some five, and so on. You may refer to chapters three and four further details.

In the interval 1, 2, 3, b5, b7, the 5th and 7th notes have been flattened. An example of a sharpened 7th chord is this: 1 3 #5 7

By now, you can see that sharps and flats are related in position to major scales. Meanwhile, you can rely on this understanding to build chords in guitar music. In fact, it is fundamental in chord theory.

Enharmonic Intervals - Same Note Intervals

Now that you understand where sharps and flats come from let's take yet another close look at the notes on the fretboard for further understanding. If you look at the chromatic scale, you'll find that there are notes or intervals that can be written in two different forms. For example, we can call F sharp (F#) "G flat" Gb, because it's the same note (enharmonic). We can also call B flat (Bb) "A sharp" A# because they are the same note.

As discussed earlier, a note can be sharp or flat, depending on how it is used. The use of sharps or flats in music is basically intended to make scale reading easy. For example, a scale that has two letters would be confusing to read. Let's say we were to spell out a scale that includes a natural A note and a flattened B note; we could write this as A, and A# or A, and Bb. But we rarely use A# in this scale notation as that would mean two As in the scale. Therefore, it's best to use its enharmonic Bb instead. From the above, you'll see why either sharps or flats are consistently used on any scale - to make the spelling of scales easier to see.

Building your Own Rhythm

The growth of any guitarist is very much dependent on mastering every new technique that they have learned before moving on to another. As I have always stated, the self-taught technique is particularly most helpful for guitarists. The diligence and commitment it demands are essential ingredients for your growth. I believe too that it is why you have picked up this book. An ideal approach is to first understand the concept behind every technique or piece of knowledge you come across in your guitar journey, then apply yourself to practice being able to use them. If a lesson seems too hard to grasp, leave it, return to the preceding steps, and build up from there again to the tough ones. You gain nothing from practice if you do not tackle the harder lessons and learn those things you find to be difficult.

With basic chords like triads and 7ths, you can begin strumming your favorite songs. You may even begin trying some licks for your music band. Meanwhile, keep an eye out for the pros in the field. You'll find more than one thing to learn from them. However, do not forget that every guitar player needs to have a unique sound, not just unique but pleasant. With the abundance of techniques and theory we've discussed so far, it is practically easier to find your feet and create your own sound.

Your fingers will develop calluses, but not to worry. They will, in fact, help you in fretting notes a lot better. Your focus should be on the fretboard and how to fret the notes of important chords. Sooner or later, the paint will wear off, and you'll get comfortable. Try and experiment on as many chords as possible; frequently visit the techniques discussed in the previous sections until you have a mastery of them.

Chapter 6

Advanced Techniques – Arpeggios

So far, you've learned how to play chord notes together as a chunk. That's just one way to play chord notes. The other is similar but involves playing the individual notes of the chords one after the other. When you play chords like this, you are applying the arpeggio technique. It is used to add special licks, more harmony, and style to your playing. Arpeggios are particularly useful in soloing. They are essential and unique techniques that a good guitar player should know.

Arpeggios require a little bit more tact and grit to get it together, but with consistent practice, you'll master them. There are various kinds of techniques in the world of arpeggios, and we'll take them one at a time, starting from the basic chords. However, it's important to first master these chords, maybe even learning as many strumming patterns as you can before getting into this. In this chapter, we'll be building heavily on our discussions in the preceding chapters.

Using Arpeggios

In arpeggios, we play the notes of a chord, one note at a time, so that they ring out separately and clearly. You can use arpeggios in complete solos on guitar over chords and progressions. The main difference between regular chord fingering and arpeggios is chords are strummed all at once as a chunk, while arpeggios involve plucking each note singly. As you can already guess, arpeggios are used with scales, chords, and chord progressions. In other words, if you are familiar with the notes of scales and chords, you'll do fine with arpeggios.

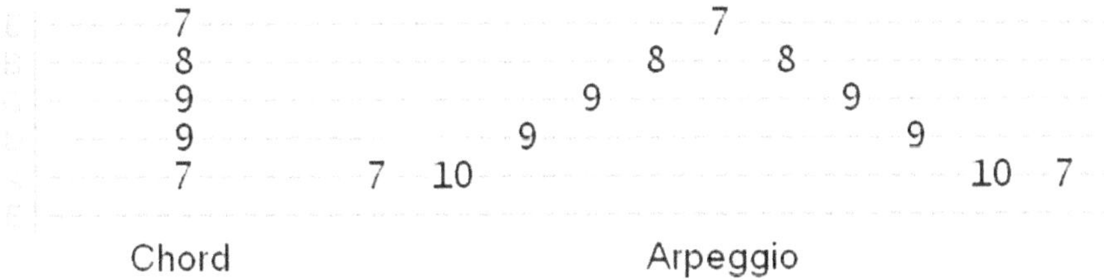

The above illustration shows the normal Emin chord and the corresponding arpeggio. So, there are as many arpeggios as there are chords: Major arpeggios, 7th arpeggios. Arpeggios are used in solos to create phases just as we have in standard scale runs. In this case, the notes of the scale or chord being played are carefully picked in such a way that harmony is built from the first note to the last. You can run a scale or chord notes back and forth, i.e., ascending arpeggios and descending arpeggios.

Arpeggios are very helpful during chord transitions. Chord changes can be made smoother with arpeggios. For example, if the chord change is from G major to F minor, you could play a G major arpeggio followed by an F minor arpeggio. By using arpeggios, you increase your flexibility and dexterity and take your soloing skills notches higher. Sooner rather than later, with continuous practice, you'll begin to handle chord progressions with so much more ease and fun.

Major Arpeggios

As the name implies, major arpeggios are played over major chords. They will help to connect your solo to the backing music. You can think of arpeggios as the "skeleton" of your solo, and when you add embellishments like scale phrases, they generally add color and flavor to your music.

Since major arpeggios are formed from major chords, the major arpeggio is made up of three similar component notes as major chords. These are The root (1) or first note, the major 3rd (3) note (gives the chord or arpeggio its major/distinguishing sound), and the perfect 5th (5) note (has a neutral sound). These notes form the basis of major arpeggios. It's important to note that you don't have to know the individual notes of every arpeggio you play since these notes are pretty much moveable across the fretboard.

Be aware also that noting the arpeggio patterns is more important than memorizing them. You may memorize a few patterns and simply move them to the appropriate root note for the chord you're playing over. This is to emphasize the relevance of knowing how to space or how one-note relates to another, in any key, and over any chord you're playing. Let's look at some essential arpeggio patterns on the guitar.

Major Arpeggio Patterns

A good way to begin building your patterns is by tackling them in the same way we would scales. Remember that each pattern has its own root position, which tells you the position of the pattern of the chord you're playing over. Begin at a comfortable tempo and increase your speed as your mastery gets better.

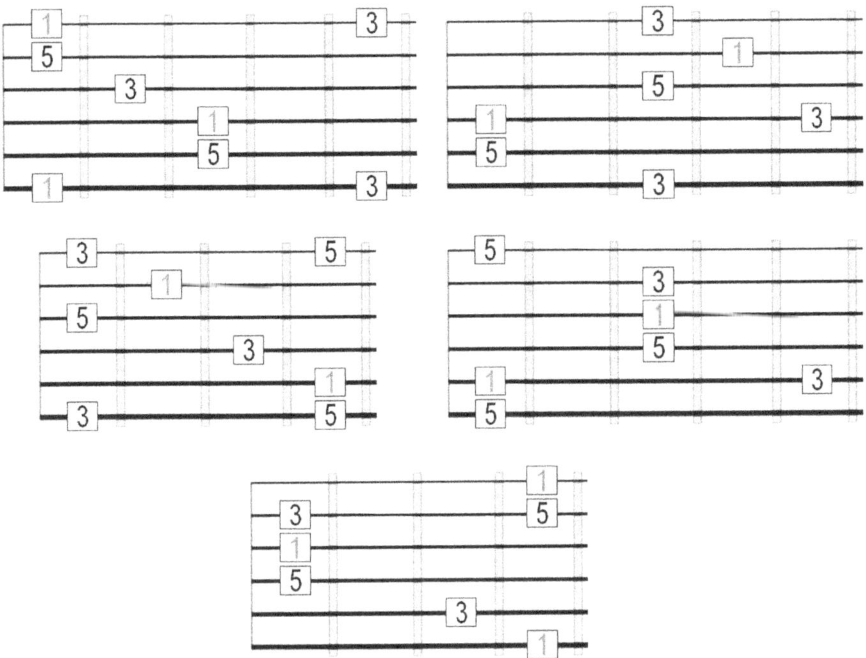

The fingering of the patterns shown above is obviously difficult, but you can use the 'rolling' technique to get your fingers accustomed to them. It's a technique used to fret two more strings on the sand fret, without distorting the sound of any of them. Place the tip of your finger on the upper string and with the pad of your finger, fret the lower string. See the illustrations below for some practical examples:

C Major Arpeggio

Note that all the roots (1) are on the note C

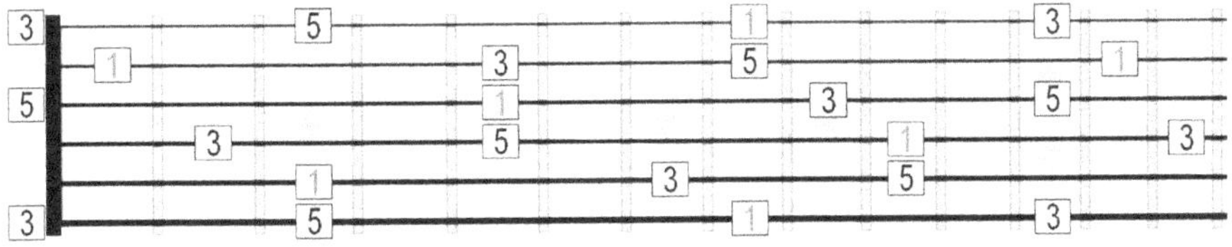

A Major Arpeggio

Just as in the C major arpeggio, all the roots are on A note.

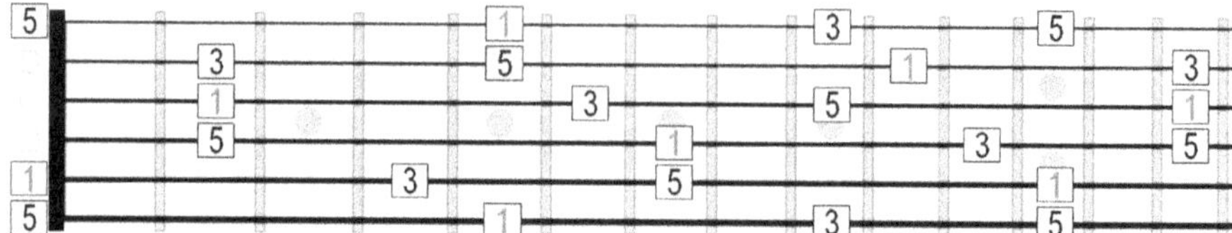

You can see that the patterns can be repeatedly played anywhere on the fretboard as long as you position the root of the patterns on the right fret. Also, you may use slides to extend your reach across the fretboard and add more melody and fluidity to your arpeggios. This might prove hard at first - and they are! But as with several other techniques you've come across before, it takes practice and patience to get arpeggios perfectly played.

Minor Arpeggios

If you've learned or mastered the major arpeggios, and you're well acquainted with the minor chord scales, you won't have issues working through the minor arpeggios. They're fundamentally the same except that the major 3rd note is flattened in the minor arpeggio. The intervals and sequence remain the same: Root (1), minor 3rd (♭3), and 5th (5). As you can see, the minor 3rd is one semitone lower than the major 3rd. So, the only necessary change that needs to be made here is to flatten the 3rd note in the corresponding major arpeggio patterns. You do this by moving one fret lower from the original major 3rd position. We can review the examples from the preceding section to see how we can practically executive this on the fretboard.

A Minor Arpeggio Patterns

Taking the root note from the A string, you can play the A minor arpeggio pattern on any suitable position on the fretboard. However, as you keep your options open, be mindful of the change in the third note. Next, you can play the arpeggio from any note of the chord, and then try linking the sequences together along the fretboard.

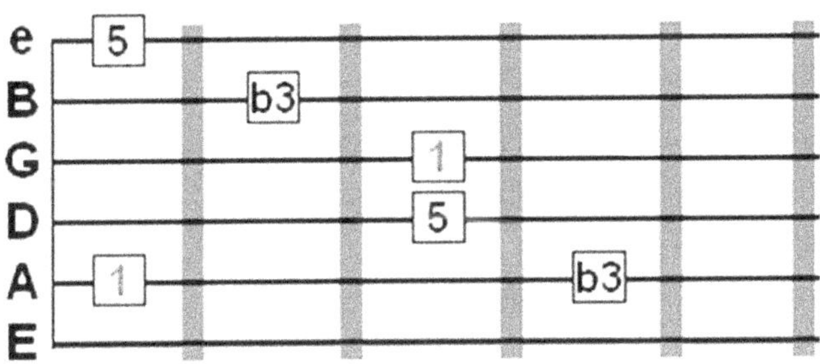

Once you get familiar with this pattern, you can get more creative in your style. You can take things a step further by using backing tracks if you can lay your hands on any. This will help you build your confidence in the patterns. At this point, I suggest you should only be focused on building your confidence with fingering the patterns discussed so far. It's not yet time to worry about speed or soloing dexterity. Get the patterns down first, and you can always build up your speed using a jam track or a metronome.

7th Arpeggios

7th arpeggios are made up of four notes, just as we have in 7th chords. The difference between them is the addition of an extra note to the major and minor triads to firm the major 7ths, as well as the 7th arpeggios. Just as the major 7th chords are richer in sound, so are the 7th arpeggios fuller in sound. Since the lessons are progressive, you'd be better off when working on these if you have mastered the arpeggio techniques preceding this one.

Since the difference is only in the addition of a fourth note to the major triad arpeggios, you don't have to learn new arpeggio fingerings for 7th arpeggios from scratch. Simply alter them to incorporate the new 7th interval.

As you can tell already, the same rules apply for 7tg arpeggios as with major arpeggios. We have the major 7th and minor 7th arpeggios.

Major 7th Arpeggio Patterns

Maj7 arpeggios are particularly used to solo over Maj7 chords. They have the following interval pattern: R 3 5 7

Root (1) - maj 3rd (3) - 5th (5) – maj 7th (7)

A Cmaj7 arpeggio, for example, will have the following notes: C, E, G, and B.

The major 7th tone, which gives the pattern its name, is positioned just one semitone below the root. Maj7 arpeggios can be played over major 7th or major triad chords. Getting this technique under your fingers advances your soloing skills further. You'll find them quite useful for playing over jazz, pop, and R&B songs. The diagram below shows the major 7th E arpeggio. Note that the root note is seated on the E string.

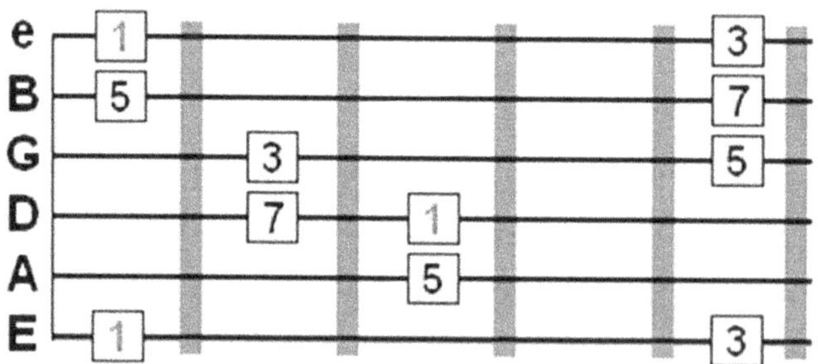

As you practice, you can solo over more than one octave for each arpeggio you play. To make your playing as practical as possible, you can play to a song or backing track or use a metronome.

Dominant 7th Arpeggios

The dominant 7th arpeggios are another set of essential arpeggios that will add flavor to your arpeggios. The 7th arpeggios are usually used to solo over dominant 7th chords or regular triad chords. Learning them expands your ability to solo over a wide range of songs. Just like the major 7th chords and arpeggios, they are also made up of four notes, i.e., R 3 5 b7 or more elaborately, Root (1) - maj 3rd (3) - 5th (5) - flat 7th (b7). The new thing here is the flattening of the 7th note. So, we simply drop the 7th down by one fret or semitone to get a dominant 7th. In this case, we call the fourth note, a flat 7th or minor 7th (b7). As an example, the dominant E 7th arpeggio would contain the following notes: E, G, B, and *b*D

See below the arpeggio pattern for soloing over a dominant 7th E chord. In terms of origin, we can also see the dominant 7th arpeggios as coming from the Mixolydian scale (the only scale with a flattened 7th note).

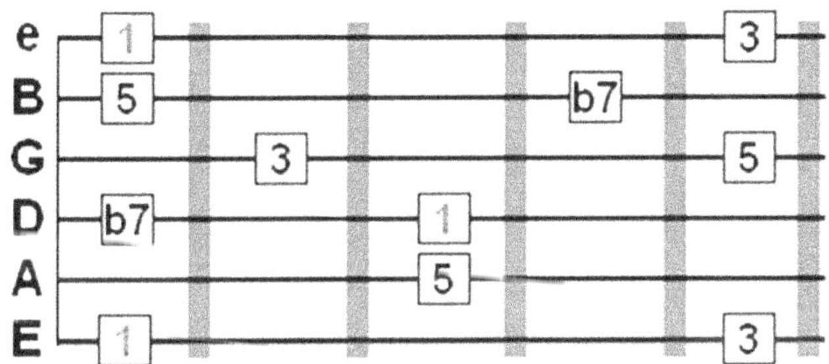

Remember that it is not necessary, to begin with, the lowest root string. You can create the pattern from any string (high E, low E, and D string, as shown in the diagram) or any octave on the fretboard. Using other known dominant 7th chords like the A dominant 7th chord, you can experiment further to master as many dominant 7th arpeggio patterns as possible.

Minor 7th Arpeggios

The arpeggios are the least popular of all the arpeggio patterns discussed so far. They are similar to the major 7th arpeggio in note structure and number except for the presence of flattened 3rd (3) and 7th notes. The pattern for min7 arpeggios is:

Root (1) - maj 3rd (3) - 5th (5)

Below is the arpeggio pattern for Emin7 Arpeggio.

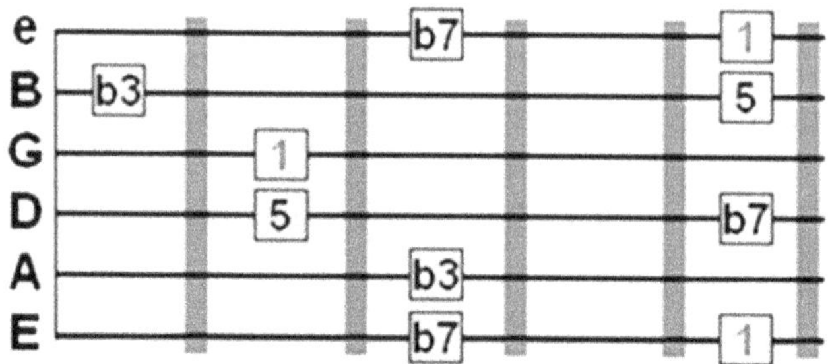

As you can guess, the minor 7th arpeggios can be used to solo over minor 7th chords or used to extend minor triad chords.

Now that you have learned the basic arpeggio patterns, you can begin trying your hand at several chords. If you want to bring in fantastic riffs and licks to your playing, arpeggios are a must. Besides, you'll be glad you took the time to learn them. Arpeggios are great for connecting lead phrases because they only include the main chord intervals.

Tips to Note:

1. Playing the entire pattern in each arpeggio isn't always necessary. You can skip or include any note of your choice, so long as you get any a good sound.

2. It's important that you are familiar with the different points within the arpeggio in case you have to improvise.

3. Typically, an arpeggio can be played over any known chord pattern

4. You can use a metronome to sustain your rhythm and tempo until you build enough confidence to play on your own.

5. You do not have to start arpeggios from the root notes. That will limit your flexibility in soloing. In fact, practicing arpeggio progressions will help broaden your creativity.

6. You don't have to use the 5th and 6th strings when playing arpeggio patterns. They can create more than enough licks from the upper strings.

Essential Arpeggio Techniques

Here we take a look at some common but essential ways to play arpeggios. Some of these are similar to what was discussed earlier in the chapter or an advanced way of using them. Generally, they all serve to add more dexterity and fluidity to your playing skills.

Rolling Technique

With this technique, you can play two or more vertical notes (notes on the same fret but different strings) using just one finger. This is usually done by playing one note (the lower note) with the tip of the finger and playing the other note with the pad of the finger. You can play in either a descending or ascending manner. The essential requirement for this technique is a great deal of flexibility in your top joints – collapsing and raising them. For example, using the index (1st) finger, you can play two vertical notes on A and D strings by placing the finger directly behind the desired fret and picking the notes with the right fingers.

The rolling technique is essential for playing arpeggios in fast succession, and also in sweep picking (discussed below). Learning this technique will be a great addition to your skills, as you'll have to deal with several vertical notes in many arpeggio patterns.

Legato Arpeggio Technique

Remember hammer-ons and pull-offs? That's what we have here. But instead of using them as we would on scales and chords, we adapt them to arpeggios. It is essential because you do not have to pick every note. Hence, it gives you the ability to run arpeggios faster than you would if you were to pick each note singly and this allows you to play several patterns repeatedly. More than that, you can apply hammer-ons and pull-offs in playing every known arpeggio pattern.

Alternate Picking Technique

Alternate picking isn't exactly a technique that improves your speed, but is primarily used by guitarists to maintain consistency and control when playing arpeggios. It simply allows you more flexibility and improvisation with your arpeggios. For a further guide on the alternate picking technique, you'll need to revisit the previous chapter under the same heading.

String Skipping

This is similar to the alternate picking technique, though it does not involve strict picking of notes. As the name implies, you skip some strings so you can play conveniently across wide note intervals. So, you avoid the linear and strict progression used in alternate picking. Incorporating this technique into your guitar licks allows you to play several lead phrases, and serves to advance your arpeggio skills.

Notice how the B string is skipped in the scale run illustrated above.

Using Arpeggios in Solos

Beyond learning and playing the corresponding arpeggio patterns for each chord you know or playing up and down a scale, there is more room for you to utilize arpeggios in more dynamic and fluid ways. Soloing over scales and chords with arpeggios is an effective way to achieve this. At this point, we are going to work through a more advanced application of arpeggios in soloing techniques.

Arpeggios can be used as lead-ins to guitar solos. In other words, in soloing, arpeggios can be used as lead-in phrases. Larger soloing phrases can then follow after the lead-in phrases on that same scale. Staggered patterns can also be introduced in guitar runs; instead of sticking to regular straight runs on a scale, you can go back and forth on the scale; take 3 tones forward and 2 back, 3 more tones forward, 2 back and so on. Arpeggios can also be used to solo over more advanced chord fingerings as in chord inversions where you alter the sequence of notes in a chord. Once more, arpeggios can be used to highlight specific chord changes within a chord progressing. Although the concepts of using arpeggios over chord inversions and highlighting chord changes are beyond the scope of this book, I encourage you still to try your hands on them after mastering the basic techniques. We will, however, dwell on extensive use of soloing in the next chapter.

Note: A lead-in phrase is a melodic sequence of notes or keys that is used to introduce a larger soloing phrase. These notes may not necessarily belong to the scale or chord they are leading in to, but will naturally flow into the notes of the soloing phrase.

Chapter 7

Soloing

Guitar solos represent one of the best techniques any guitarist can incorporate into playing the guitar. The majority of, if not all, rhythm guitarists use solos at length, so do guitar players who play popular music such as bass, swing, rock, metal, and blues. In fact, without solos, guitar music is regarded as incomplete and limited. Solos bring in the flavor and special licks that make a unique sound. To save words, you need to get the soloing skill under your belt.

A guitar solo is used when you need to play specific notes on the fretboard. Unlike chords that only allow the playing of the notes in a scale as a whole stack, solos incorporate the picking of individual notes in a scale or chord, making it possible to produce appealing melodies and harmonies that would otherwise not be possible with just strumming. Guitar solos involve virtuoso techniques and a lot of improvisation. Think of solos as the magical effect of Spanish guitarists in the 19th and 20th centuries.

Before we delve deeper, let's consider some important concepts that embellish your soloing. The first is selecting a key for your solo, especially if you are going to be soloing over a chord. Begin your solo by selecting a key for the chord or scale you want to play over. Usually, the root note of the chord is used as the key. For example, to solo over the C Major chord, the appropriate key or scale would be the C major scale. However, this does not mean that you must always begin soloing on the root note. You have the opportunity to be creative and use improvisation, but you need to stay in tune.

Another is phrasing. Phrasing introduces structure in your soloing and makes it interesting. Instead of just running up and down a scale, you can play your notes in licks in short separated runs – like having a conversation that is broken into sentences with strategic pauses and voice inflections. Playing solos with phrases prevents you from sounding monotonous and makes your runs more articulate. The bottom line is building inflections into your solos improves your sound.

The next is regarding repeating the theme in your solos. The beauty of repeating themes is the cohesive feel they give as you solo. Although repeating themes aren't always a necessity, having them within your solo at the right time adds to the uniqueness of your sound. They'll also help in phrasing because it leaves natural pauses in your solo. The essence of these little touches is to make your sound as interesting as possible. For example, a lot of guitarists approach arpeggios and soloing the same way as you would a scale. But it shouldn't be so. The pauses and repetition of notes are necessary to keep your audience engaged and tuned in to your music.

The next technique is building your solos dynamically. Instead of running monotonously through every scale or chord, you could start by building your solo gradually. Begin with a low tempo, progress at a faster pace, then end naturally with a fade or higher intensity. Some songs require a unique feel and are best played as solos. Bringing out the beauty in this kind of song depends on the licks you incorporate into your solo. Finally, bear in mind that you'll need to play over chord changes - several of them if you want to build your solos. This means you should be very conversant with the notes of every chord you'll be playing.

Soloing Over Chord Progressions

This is one of the most valuable skills you can add to your portfolio as a guitarist. Crucial to your success in this regard are the key ways to connect your solo to the chords you're playing. We will be discussing these subsequently.

Finding Chord Tones with Chord Shapes

As I earlier mentioned, the first step to learning how to solo over chords is to try and find the related notes of the chords you're playing over on the fretboard. They help you stay within the neighborhood of the tones of chords you`re soloing over and prevent you from drifting into dissonance. Some players even prefer to end guitar phrases on the root key or note to achieve a tying –up feel on every solo. Begin by visualizing the chord progression in the form of regular chord shapes. This is your easiest way of finding the chord tones. For example, let`s begin with the E and A form barre chord shapes, which I believe you're already familiar with. Remember, as you play, your aim is to get familiar with these chord shapes and their location in the progression.

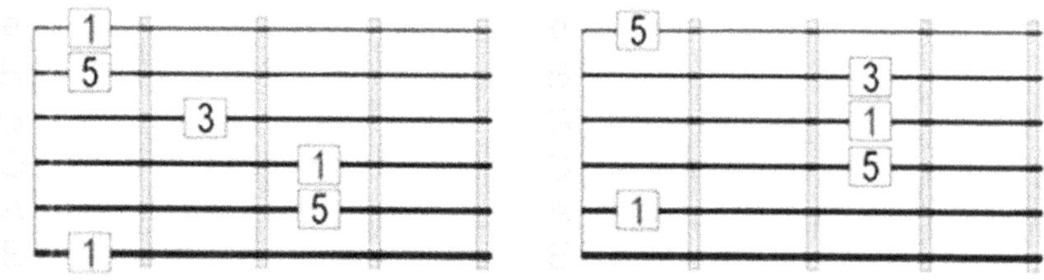

E form major chord   A form major chord

Once you are able to identify the chord tones for each chord shape, you can then start playing the solos on each chord, one note at a time. After you master this, you may proceed to play connecting the chords in your solo. At this point, your knowledge of the notes on the fretboard will come real handy.

Chord Changes Are Easier With Arpeggios

Arpeggios can be used to transition from one chord to another. Because of the embellishment that arpeggios bring to guitar music, they can easily serve as a skeleton or scaffolding to build chord changes. However, in selecting notes for the arpeggios, we must stick to related or relevant note, so we don't play out of context. This should not be difficult because chords are the basis for arpeggios, only that this time, we engage the notes of the chords in arpeggios for phrasing and lead-ins.

Before you dig into this technique, you might want to take some time and build up your skills on the basic arpeggio patterns available.

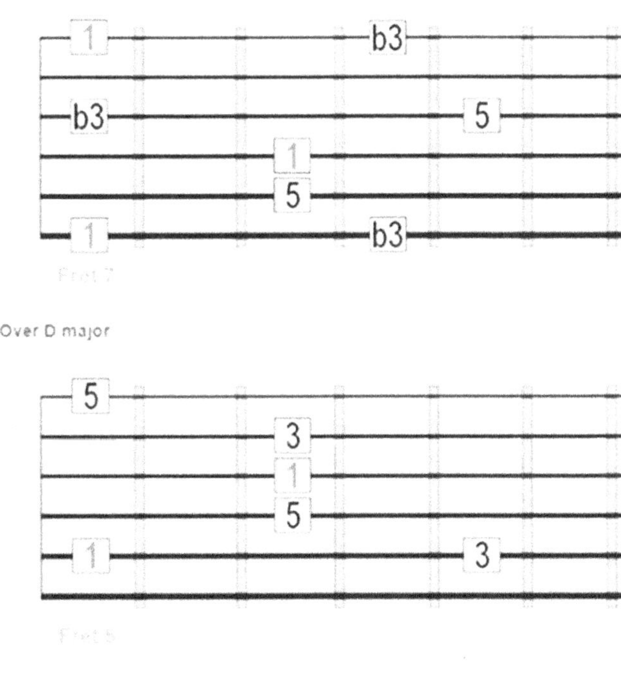

A major Chord

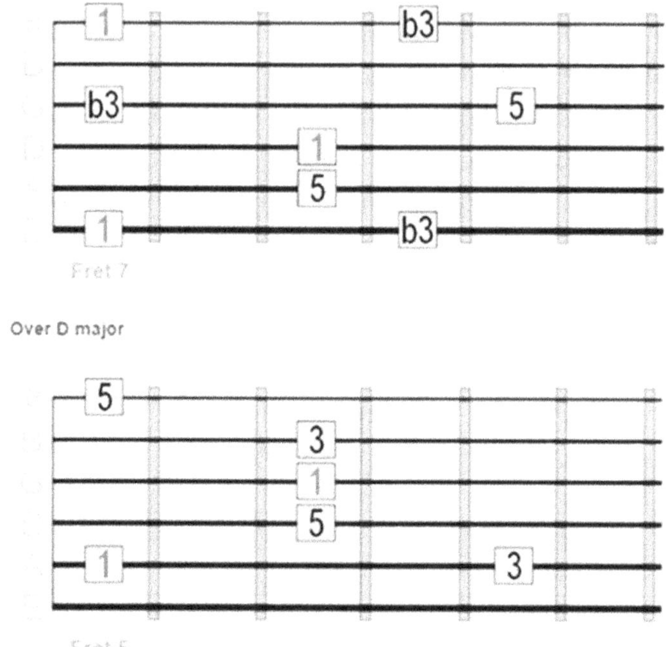

E major chord

As before, once you are able to identify the chord tones, you can use the related arpeggios to move smoothly from one chord to another. I leave you to your creativity here. As an exercise, try figuring out notes for the arpeggio you need to connect the chords. This is good training for your ear. A good hint here would be to play the last note of the first or current arpeggio followed immediately after by the first note of the next arpeggio. Remember that each arpeggio should contain the same notes as the parent chord you are playing over. Meanwhile, always keep your chord changes close in proximity and pitch to make the flow seamless.

Identify Chord Tones within Scale Patterns

Another method for soloing when playing chords over changes is by identifying the root chord notes of every key on a scale. We achieve this by looking inside the scale pattern of the scale we are playing. This method is a bit more sophisticated than the previous two. To begin with, bear in mind that most guitar progressions are connected to the major scale. Each note in a major scale represents the root of a new chord. For example, the third note of the C major scale is E, and it is the root note of the E major chord. So, on a heptatonic (7 notes) scale, we can isolate a sequence of 7 different chords from within the scale. Roman numerals are used to symbolize these chords (upper case for major chords and lower case for minor chords).

Scale Tones	1	2	3	4	5	6	7
Related Chords	I	ii	iii	IV	V	vi	vii

Note: *Remembering this table means you know the formula for a lot of chord progressions over which you'll be soloing.*

Chords	I	ii	iii	IV	V	vi	vii
Scale Tones used	1, 3, and 5	2, 4, and 6	3, 5 and 7	4, 6, and 1	5, 7, and 2	6, 1, and 3	7, 2, and 4

With this illustration, identifying the root note of each chord is easy. The root of the chord (I), for example, is the first note in the scale, while that of the second is the 2nd note of the scale and so on. Next, we find out which scale tone is used for each of the chords. The first chord (I) uses 1, 3, and 5, while the third (iii) uses 3, 5, and 7 intervals. With the aid of the table above, you can commit these sequences to memory. The benefit you get from doing this is knowing exactly where the chord tones for each chord in a typical major key progression are positioned. With this understanding, your soloing over several chord progression becomes a lot easier. The main idea behind this method is being able to find the chord tones for the chords in any progression by looking into the scales that constitute these chords. The method is complicated, but it is more detailed, and it gives you a big picture view of soloing over chord changes.

Using Arpeggios in Guitar Solos

As of now, you already know the importance of arpeggios and solos in guitar music. More importantly, you know that each is a must-have for every guitarist out there. By adding arpeggios to your solos and scale phrases, you make them more appealing musically. Besides, the licks and jams you create are enriched with arpeggios in the mix. The best way to get this done is to visualize arpeggios within every scale pattern you play. You may refer to our previous discussion on arpeggios in scales and chords in the previous chapter for more comprehensive information on the subject. One of the major importance of arpeggios is in connecting chords with your solo. Let's look at some examples using **major** and **minor scales.**

Recall that we can isolate seven different chords from the major scale. Another way of looking at it is we can derive seven related arpeggios from a given major scale pattern. So, during chord changes, we carefully select a related arpeggio to the use of the transitions. The importance here is to ensure that the chord changes are preceded and succeed with the correct or related arpeggios. Effectively, this practice offers a great way to connect your solo to the chord changes. As a basic example, let's try changing from B minor (ii) to A major (I). But first, let's establish the fingering of these chords.

The A major chord is an (I) chord pattern that has the formula (1 3 5) while the minor B chord is an (ii) chord with the formula (1 ♭3 5). See the illustration below for further details.

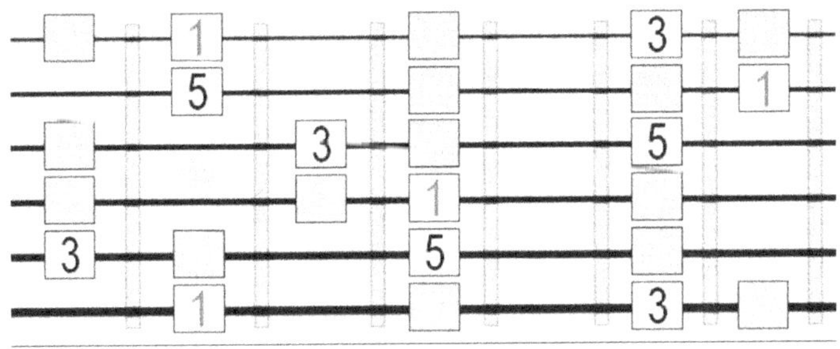

A major (I) chord

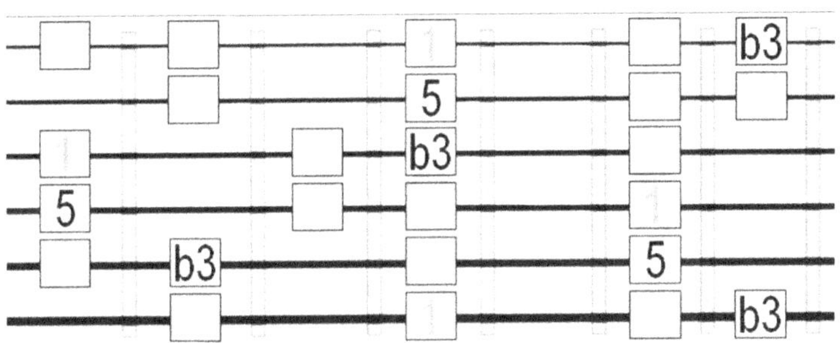

B minor (ii) chord

These are triad chords, so changing from between both chords will be less complicated as the notes are not that different, and are easy to memorize. From here, you can try your hands on other chord changes, but essentially, be mindful of the chord tones as you solo. If you get it right, you will enjoy what you're playing.

Tips for Effective Soloing

1. Be sure to phrase your solos. Avoid continuous runs without any inflections

2. Search out the key of the scale or chord before inserting your solo.

3. Try to end your phrases on the root note. It adds color and depth to the key.

4. Incorporate as many arpeggio techniques as possible to your solo

5. You may need to sing what you play, especially in lead-ins.

6. When selecting your chord shapes, try and choose the ones that are in close proximity to the previous and next chords.

7. Keep the practice going, sooner rather than later, your patience will begin to pay off

8. To make your sound interesting, you need to try out many arpeggio patterns and techniques available and also create your own arpeggios.

Conclusion

Moving On From Here

I must say that the concepts discussed within this book are not exhaustive, even though I stretched a lot of the discussions to cover more than enough ground for the intermediate player who's looking to be a pro. Once again, I congratulate you for sticking with me through to the end. I hope you find this resource very helpful in your guitar journey.

Beyond all that has been taught in this book, I encourage you to try your hand on more lessons and topics which you feel weren't sufficiently addressed here. By and large, I do hope that the answers you seek are well elaborated within the pages of this book.

References

1. Olav Turvund (2005), Music theory for guitar http://www.torvund.net/guitar/Theory/index.asp (2 of 2)10.01.2005 00:57:43

2. Catherine Schmidt-Jones (2016), Music theory for guitar. http://cnx.org/content/col12060/1.4/

3. Dale Cotton (2010), Practical music theory for guitar players. Version 1.67. http://daystarvisions.com/Music/index.html

4. Mike Beatham (2019), Guitar Theory Lessons You Can Actually Understand. FretJam. http://www.fretjam.com/guitar-theory-lessons.html

5. Move Forward Guitar LLC (2016) Music theory for Guitar. http://www.moveforwardguitar.com/

6. Nate Savage (2019), Soloing Tips. Guitarworld. https://www.guitarworld.com/lessons/session-guitar-10-life-saving-soloing-tips

7. National Guitar Academy. The 7 Steps To Guitar Mastery. http://www.nationalguitaracademy.com/

8. National Guitar Academy. Chords. https://nationalguitaracademy.com/how-to-play-a-guitar-solo/

9. Desi Serna (2013) fretboard theory volume II. http://guitar-music-theory.com/

10. Nate Savage (2019), Lead Guitar Quick Start Series.
    https://www.guitarlessons.com/guitar-lessons/lead-guitar-
    quick-start-series/